Caring for
School Age Children

Caring for
School Age Children

Phyllis M. Click and Jennifer Parker

Australia • Brazil • Japan • Korea • Mexico • Singapore • Spain • United Kingdom • United States

DELMAR
CENGAGE Learning™

Caring for School Age Children:
Professional Enhancement Series

Phyllis M. Click, Jennifer Parker

NOTICE TO THE READER
The authors and Delmar affirm that the Web site URLs referenced herein were accurate at the time of printing. However, due to the fluid nature of the Internet, we cannot guarantee their accuracy for the life of the edition.

For product information and technology assistance, contact us at **Cengage Learning Customer & Sales Support, 1-800-354-9706**

For permission to use material from this text or product, submit all requests online at **www.cengage.com/permissions** Further permissions questions can be emailed to **permissionrequest@cengage.com**

Library of Congress Catalog Card Number: 2005000019
ISBN-13: 978-1-4018-9775-8
ISBN-10: 1-4018-9775-4

Delmar
10 Davis Drive
Belmont, CA 94002-3098
USA

Cengage Learning is a leading provider of customized learning solutions with office locations around the globe, including Singapore, the United Kingdom, Australia, Mexico, Brazil, and Japan. Locate your local office at:
www.cengage.com/global

Cengage Learning products are represented in Canada by Nelson Education, Ltd.

To learn more about Delmar, visit **www.cengage.com/delmar**

Purchase any of our products at your local college store or at our preferred online store **www.ichapters.com**

Printed in Canada
6 7 8 9 10 11 10 09

TABLE OF CONTENTS

This tool was developed to help you, the budding teacher and/or child care provider, as you move into your first classroom. The editors at Thomson Delmar Learning encourage and appreciate your feedback on this or any of our other products. Go to www.earlychilded.delmar.com and click on the "Professional Enhancement series feedback" link to let us know what you think.

INTRODUCTION

Throughout a college program of preparation to become an early childhood educator, students take many courses and read many textbooks. Their knowledge grows as they accumulate ideas from lectures, reading, experiences, and discussions. When they finish their coursework, graduate, and move into their first teaching positions, students often leave behind some of the books they have used. The hope is, however, that they will take with them the important ideas from their classes and books as they begin their own professional practice.

More experienced colleagues or mentors sometimes support teachers in their first teaching positions, helping them make the transition between college classroom and being responsible for a group of young children. Other times, new teachers are left to travel their own paths, relying on their own resources. Whatever your situation, this professional enhancement guide is designed to provide reminders of what you have learned, as well as resources to help you make sense of and apply that knowledge.

Teachers of young children are under great pressure today. From families, there are the demands for support in their difficult tasks of child-rearing in today's fast-paced and changing world. Some families become so overwhelmed with the tasks of parenting that they seem to leave too much responsibility on the shoulders of teachers and caregivers. From administrators and institutions, there are expectations that sometimes seem overwhelming. Teachers are being held accountable for children's learning in ways unprecedented even in the recent past. Public scrutiny has led to insistence on teaching practices that may seem contrary to the best interests of children or their teachers. New teachers may find themselves caught between the realities of the schools or centers where they find themselves, and their own philosophies and ideals of working with children. When faced with such dilemmas, it is important for these individuals to be able to fall back and reflect on what they know of best practices, renewing their professional determination to make appropriate decisions for children.

These books provide similar tools for that reflection:

- tips for getting off to a great start in your new environment
- information about typical developmental patterns of children from birth through school age
- suggestions for materials that promote development for children from infancy through the primary grades
- tools to assist teachers in observing children and gathering data to help set appropriate goals for individual children
- guides for planning appropriate classroom experiences and sample lesson plans
- tips for introducing children to the joys of literacy
- a summary of the key ideas about Developmentally Appropriate Practice, the process of decision-making that allows teachers to provide optimum environments for children from birth through school age
- resources for teachers for professional development
- ideas for where you can access lists of other resources
- case studies of relevant, realistic situations you may face, as well as best practices for successfully navigating them
- insight into issues and trends facing early childhood educators today.
- the book has been designed for useability. The margins have been enlarged to enable users to use this space for notes.

Becoming a teacher is a process of continuing to grow, learn, reflect, and discover through experience. Having these resources may help you along your way. Good luck on your journey!

REFLECTIONS FOR GROWING TEACHERS

Teachers spend most of their time working with young children and their families. During the day, questions and concerns arise and decisions have to be made, meaning teachers must always be reflective about their work. Too often, teachers believe they are too busy to spend time thinking, but experienced professional teachers have learned that reflection sustains their best work. Growing teachers need to regularly take time to consider the questions and concerns that arise from their practice. Some teachers use journals to keep track of the process.

Use these questions to begin your reflection and then add to them with questions from your own experience. Remember, these are not questions to be answered once and forgotten—come back often.

QUESTIONS FOR REFLECTION

This day would have been better if _____

_____

_____

I think I need to know more about _____

_____

_____

One new thing I think I will try this week is _____

_____

_____

The highlight of this week was _____

_____

_____

The observations this week made me think more about _____

_____

_____

I think my favorite creative activity this year was _____

_____

_____

One area where my teaching is changing is _____

_____

_____

One area where my teaching needs to change is _____

_____

_____

I just do not understand why _____

_____

_____

I loved my job this week when _____

_____

_____

I hated my job this week when _____

_____

One thing I can try to make better next week is _____

_____

The funniest thing I heard a child say this week was _____

_____

The family member I feel most comfortable with is _____

_____

And I think the reason for that is _____

_____

The family member I feel least comfortable with is _____

_____

And I think the reason for that is _____

_____

The biggest gains in learning have been made by _____

_____

And I think that this is because _____

_____

I am working on a bad habit of _____

_____

_____

Has my attitude about teaching changed this year? Why? _____

_____

_____

What have I done lately to spark the children's imagination and creativity? _____

_____

_____

One quote that I like to keep in mind is _____

_____

_____

Dealing with _____ is the most difficult thing I had to face recently

because _____

_____

My teaching style has been most influenced by _____

_____

_____

In thinking more about my curriculum, I believe_____

_____

_____

If I were going to advise a new teacher, the most helpful piece of advice would be

_____

_____

I have been trying to facilitate friendships among the children by _____

_____

_____

I really need to start _____

_____

_____

I used to _____ but now I _____

_____

_____

The child who has helped me learn the most is _____

_____

I learned _____

_____

I have grown in my communication by _____

_____

_____

The best thing I have learned by observing is _____

_____

_____

I still do not understand why _____

_____

_____

One mistake I used to make that I do not make any longer is _____

_____

_____

When next year starts, one thing I will do more of is _____

_____

_____

When next year starts, one thing I will not do is _____

_____

_____

_____

_____

_____

One way I can help my children feel more competent is _____

_____

_____

_____

_____

Something I enjoy that I could share with my class is _____

_____

_____

_____

_____

When children have difficulty sharing, I _____

_____

_____

_____

_____

Adapted from Nilsen, B. A., *Week by Week: Documenting the Development of Young Children* (3rd ed.), published by Thomson Delmar Learning.

TIPS FOR SUCCESS

Remember that you are a role model for the children. They are constantly watching how you dress, what you say, and what you do.

BE A PROFESSIONAL

- Dress conservatively and follow your employer's clothing expectations (which could include wearing closed-toe shoes to be safe and active with children and wearing clean, modest, and comfortable clothing).

- Be prepared and on time.

- Avoid excessive absences.

- Use appropriate language with children and adults.

- Be positive when talking to parents and show that you are forming a positive relationship with their child; "catch children doing something right" and share those accomplishments. Challenges with children can be discussed after you have established trust with the parents.

BE A TEAM PLAYER

- Rely on team members to help you learn the parameters of your new position.

- Do not be afraid to ask questions or for guidance from teammates.

- Show your support and be responsible.

- Step in to do your share of the work; do not expect others to clean up after you.

- Be of assistance to others whenever possible.

- Respect others' ideas and avoid telling them how to do things.

- Strive to balance your ability to make decisions by following the lead of others.

LEARN ABOUT CHILDREN

- Be aware of their development physically, socially, emotionally, and cognitively.

- Assess children's development and plan curriculum that will enhance it.

- Be aware that children will test you! (Children, especially school age, will expect that you do not know the rules and may try to convince you to let them do things that were not previously allowed.).

- Never hesitate to double-check something with teammates when in doubt.

- Use positive management techniques with children.

MANAGEMENT TECHNIQUES FOR GAINING CHILDREN'S COOPERATION

There are myriad techniques that will help children cooperate. Children need respectful reminders of expectations and adult support in performing to those expectations. Be sure that your expectations are age appropriate and individually appropriate. These techniques are more preventive in nature:

- Use positive phrases and state exactly what you expect children to do. "Stand by the door" is more effective that "Don't go outside until everyone is ready."

- Avoid "no" and "don't." Be clear about what it is you want children to do, not what you do not want them to do.

- Sequence directions using "When-then." For example, "When things are put away where they belong, then we can go outside."

■ Stay close. Merely standing near children can be enough to help them manage their behavior. Be aware, however, that if you are talking to another adult, children may act out because they know they do not have your attention.

■ Offer sufficient and appropriate choices. Children need a variety of activities that interest them and that will create opportunities for success.

GETTING STARTED

There is always an array of information to learn when starting in a new position of working with children. Use this fill-in-the-blank section to customize this resource book to your specific environment.

What are the school's or center's hours of operation?

On school days: _____

_____

_____

On vacation days: _____

_____

_____

What is the basic daily schedule and what are my responsibilities during each time segment?

_____

_____

_____

_____

_____

_____

_____

What are the procedures for checking children in and out of the program?

_____

_____

_____

_____

Do I call if I have to be absent? Who is my contact?

Name:_____

Phone Number: _____

What is the dress code for employees?

_____

_____

_____

For what basic health and safety practices will I be responsible? Where are the materials stored for this? (Bleach, gloves, etc.)

Sanitizing tables: _____

_____

_____

_____

Cleaning and maintaining of equipment and materials: _____

_____

_____

_____

What are the emergency procedures?

Mildly injured child: _____

_____

_____

_____

_____

Earthquake/Tornado: _____

_____

_____

_____

_____

_____

Fire: _____

_____

_____

_____

_____

First aid: _____

_____

_____

_____

Other: _____

_____

_____

_____

DEVELOPMENTAL MILESTONES BY AGE

Whether you are working with infants, toddlers, preschoolers, or primary-aged children, a teacher's first requirement is to have knowledge about how children develop and learn. In your college program, you no doubt studied child development. The following is a shortened version of the universal steps most children go through as they develop. Some children will move easily from one step to another, while other children move forward in one area but lag behind in others. Use these milestones as a guide for arranging an environment or planning activities in your room.

FIVE- TO SEVEN-YEAR-OLDS

- More independent of parents, able to take care of their own physical needs.

- Rely upon their peer group for self-esteem, have two or three best friends.

- Learn to share and take turns, participate in group games.

- Are eager to learn and succeed in school.

- Have a sense of duty and develop a conscience.

- Are less aggressive and resolve conflicts with words.

- Begin to see others' point of view.

- Can sustain interest for long periods of time.

- Can remember and relate past events.

- Have good muscle control and can manage simple tools.

- Have a high energy level.

Child's Name _____   Age _____

Observer _____   Date _____

Developmental Checklist (by five years)

Does the child . . .	Yes	No	Sometimes
1. Walk backward, heel to toe?	☐	☐	☐
2. Walk up and down stairs, alternating feet?	☐	☐	☐
3. Cut on line?	☐	☐	☐
4. Print some letters?	☐	☐	☐
5. Point to and name three shapes?	☐	☐	☐
6. Raise up on arms, lifting head and chest, when placed on stomach?	☐	☐	☐
7. Demonstrate number concepts to four or five?	☐	☐	☐
8. Cut food with a knife: celery, sandwich?	☐	☐	☐
9. Lace shoes?	☐	☐	☐
10. Read from story picture book—in other words, tell story by looking at pictures?	☐	☐	☐
11. Draw a person with three to six body parts?	☐	☐	☐
12. Play and interact with other children; engage in dramatic play that is close to reality?	☐	☐	☐
13. Build complex structures with blocks or other building materials?			
14. Respond to simple three-step directions: "Give me the pencil, put the book on the table, and hold the comb in your hand"?	☐	☐	☐
15. Respond correctly when asked to show penny, nickel, and dime?	☐	☐	☐
16. Ask "How" questions?	☐	☐	☐
17. Respond verbally to "Hi" and "How are you"?	☐	☐	☐
18. Tell about events using past and future tenses?	☐	☐	☐

Use conjunctions to string words and phrases together—for example, "I saw a bear and a zebra and a giraffe at the zoo?"

DEVELOPMENTAL ALERTS

Check with a health care provider or early childhood specialist if, by the *fifth* birthday, the child *does not*:

- State own name in full.

- Recognize simple shapes: circle, square, triangle.

- Catch a large ball when bounced (have child's vision checked).

- Speak so as to be understood by strangers (have child's hearing checked).

- Have good control of posture and movement.

- Hop on one foot.

- Appear interested in, and responsive to, surroundings.

- Respond to statements without constantly asking to have them repeated.

- Dress self with minimal adult assistance; manage buttons, zippers.

- Take care of own toilet needs; have good bowel and bladder control with infrequent accidents.

Child's Name _____ Age _____

Observer _____ Date _____

Developmental Checklist (by six years)

Does the child . . .	Yes	No	Sometimes
1. Walk across a balance beam?	☐	☐	☐
2. Skip with alternating feet?	☐	☐	☐
3. Hop for several seconds on one foot?	☐	☐	☐
4. Cut out simple shapes?	☐	☐	☐
5. Copy own first name?	☐	☐	☐
6. Show well-established handedness; demonstrate consistent right- or left-handedness?	☐	☐	☐
7. Sort objects on one or more dimensions: color, shape, or function?	☐	☐	☐
8. Name most letters and numerals?	☐	☐	☐
9. Count by rote to 10; know what number comes next?	☐	☐	☐
10. Dress self completely; tie bows?	☐	☐	☐
11. Brush teeth unassisted?	☐	☐	☐
12. Have some concept of clock time in relation to daily schedule?	☐	☐	☐

Developmental Checklist, continued

Does the child . . .	Yes	No	Sometimes
13. Cross street safely?	☐	☐	☐
14. Draw a person with head, trunk, legs, arms, and features; often add clothing details?	☐	☐	☐
15. Play simple board games?	☐	☐	☐
16. Engage in cooperative play with other children, involving group decisions, role assignments, rule observance?	☐	☐	☐
17. Use construction toys, such as Legos®, blocks, to make recognizable structures?	☐	☐	☐
18. Do 15-piece puzzles?	☐	☐	☐
19. Use all grammatical structures: pronouns, plurals, verb tenses, conjunctions?	☐	☐	☐
20. Use complex sentences: carry on conversations?	☐	☐	☐

DEVELOPMENTAL ALERTS

Check with a health care provider or early childhood specialist if, by the *sixth* birthday, the child *does not*:

- Alternate feet when walking up and down stairs.
- Speak in a moderate voice; neither too loud, too soft, too high, too low.
- Follow simple directions in stated order: "Please go to the cupboard, get a cup, and bring it to me."
- Use four to five words in acceptable sentence structure.
- Cut on a line with scissors.
- Sit still and listen to an entire short story (five to seven minutes).
- Maintain eye contact when spoken to (unless this is a cultural taboo).
- Play well with other children.
- Perform most self-grooming tasks independently: brush teeth, wash hands and face.

Child's Name _____   Age _____
Observer _____   Date _____

Developmental Checklist (by seven years)

Does the child ...	Yes	No	Sometimes
1. Concentrate on completing puzzles and board games?	☐	☐	☐
2. Ask many questions?	☐	☐	☐
3. Use correct verb tenses, word order, and sentence structure in conversation?	☐	☐	☐
4. Correctly identify right and left hands?	☐	☐	☐
5. Make friends easily?	☐	☐	☐
6. Show some control of anger, using words instead of physical aggression?	☐	☐	☐
7. Participate in play that requires teamwork and rule observance?	☐	☐	☐
8. Seek adult approval for efforts?	☐	☐	☐
9. Enjoy reading and being read to?	☐	☐	☐
10. Use pencil to write words and numbers?	☐	☐	☐
11. Sleep undisturbed through the night?	☐	☐	☐
12. Catch a tennis ball, walk across balance beam, hit ball with bat?	☐	☐	☐
13. Plan and carry out simple projects with minimal adult help?	☐	☐	☐
14. Tie own shoes?	☐	☐	☐
15. Draw pictures with greater detail and sense of proportion?	☐	☐	☐
16. Care for own personal needs with some adult supervision? Wash hands? Brush teeth? Use toilet? Dress self?	☐	☐	☐
17. Show some understanding of cause-and-effect concepts?	☐	☐	☐

DEVELOPMENTAL ALERTS

Check with a health care provider or early childhood specialist if, by the *seventh* birthday, the child *does not*:

- Show signs of ongoing growth: increasing height and weight; continuing motor development, such as running, jumping, balancing.

- Show some interest in reading and trying to reproduce letters, especially own name.

- Follow simple, multiple-step directions: "Finish your book, put it on the shelf, and then get your coat on."

- Follow through with instructions and complete simple tasks: putting dishes in the sink, picking up clothes, finishing a puzzle. *Note*: All children forget. Task incompletion is not a problem unless a child *repeatedly* leaves tasks unfinished.

- Begin to develop alternatives to excessive use of inappropriate behaviors in order to get own way.

- Develop a steady decrease in tension-type behaviors that may have developed with starting school: repeated grimacing or facial tics; eye twitching; grinding of teeth; regressive soiling or wetting; frequent stomachaches; refusing to go to school.

8- TO 10-YEAR-OLDS

- Need parental guidance and support for school achievement.

- Competition is common.

- Pronounced gender differences in interests, same gender cliques formed.

- Spend a lot of time in physical game playing.

- Academic achievement is important.

- Begin to develop moral values, make value judgments about own behavior.

- Are aware of the importance of belonging.

- Strong gender role conformation.

- Begin to think logically and to understand cause and effect.

- Use language to communicate ideas and can use abstract words.

- Can read but ability varies.

- Realize importance of physical skills in determining status among peers.

Child's Name _____   Age _____
Observer _____   Date _____

Developmental Checklist (by eight and nine years)

Does the child . . .	Yes	No	Sometimes
1. Have energy to play, continuing growth, few illnesses?	☐	☐	☐
2. Use pencil in a deliberate and controlled manner?	☐	☐	☐
3. Express relatively complex thoughts in a clear and logical fashion?	☐	☐	☐
4. Carry out multiple four- to five-step instructions?	☐	☐	☐
5. Become less easily frustrated with own performance?	☐	☐	☐
6. Interact and play cooperatively with other children?	☐	☐	☐
7. Show interest in creative expression—telling stories, jokes, writing, drawing, singing?	☐	☐	☐
8. Use eating utensils with ease?	☐	☐	☐
9. Have a good appetite? Show interest in trying new foods?	☐	☐	☐
10. Know how to tell time?	☐	☐	☐
11. Have control of bowel and bladder functions?	☐	☐	☐
12. Participate in some group activities—games, sports, plays?	☐	☐	☐
13. Want to go to school? Seem disappointed if must miss a day?	☐	☐	☐
14. Demonstrate beginning skills in reading, writing, and math?	☐	☐	☐
15. Accept responsibility and complete work independently?	☐	☐	☐
16. Handle stressful situations without becoming overly upset?	☐	☐	☐

DEVELOPMENTAL ALERTS

Check with a health care provider or early childhood specialist if, by the *eighth* birthday, the child *does not*:

- Attend to the task at hand; show longer periods of sitting quietly, listening, responding appropriately.

- Follow through on simple instructions.

- Go to school willingly most days (of concern are excessive complaints about stomachaches or headaches when getting ready for school).

- Make friends (observe closely to see if the child plays alone most of the time or withdraws consistently from contact with other children).

- Sleep soundly most nights (frequent and recurring nightmares or bad dreams are usually at a minimum at this age).

- Seem to see or hear adequately at times (squints, rubs eyes excessively, asks frequently to have things repeated).

- Handle stressful situations without undue emotional upset (excessive crying, sleeping or eating disturbances, withdrawal, frequent anxiety).

- Assume responsibility for personal care (dressing, bathing, feeding self) most of the time.

- Show improved motor skills.

DEVELOPMENTAL ALERTS

Check with a health care provider or early childhood specialist if, by the *ninth* birthday, the child *does not*:

- Exhibit a good appetite and continued weight gain (some children, especially girls, may already begin to show early signs of an eating disorder).

- Experience fewer illnesses.

- Show improved motor skills, in terms of agility, speed, and balance.

- Understand abstract concepts and use complex thought processes to problem-solving.

- Enjoy school and the challenge of learning.

- Follow through on multiple-step instructions.

- Express ideas clearly and fluently.

- Form friendships with other children and enjoy participating in group activities.

11- TO 13-YEAR-OLDS

- Parental influence is decreasing and some rebellion may occur.

- Peer group is important and sets standards for behavior.

- Worry about what others think.

- Choose friends based on common interests.

- Gender differences in interests.

- Develop awareness and interest in opposite gender.

- Begin to question adult authority.

- Often reluctant to attend child care; are bored or think they can care for themselves.

- May be moody and experience stress over physical changes of puberty.

- May be rebellious as they seek their own identity.

- Can think abstractly and apply logic to solving problems.

- Have a good command of spoken and written language.

- Girls develop gender characteristics, boys begin a growth spurt.

- Early maturing is related to a positive self-image.

- Able to master physical skills necessary for playing games.

Child's Name _____   Age _____

Observer _____   Date _____

Developmental Checklist (by 10 and 11 years)

Does the child . . .	Yes	No	Sometimes
1. Continue to increase in height and weight?	☐	☐	☐
2. Exhibit improving coordination: running, climbing, riding a bike, writing?	☐	☐	☐
3. Handle stressful situations without becoming overly upset or violent?	☐	☐	☐
4. Construct sentences using reasonably correct grammar: nouns, adverbs, verbs, adjectives?	☐	☐	☐
5. Understand concepts of time, distance, space, volume?	☐	☐	☐
6. Have one or two "best friends"?	☐	☐	☐
7. Maintain friendships over time?	☐	☐	☐
8. Approach challenges with a reasonable degree of self-confidence?	☐	☐	☐
9. Play cooperatively and follow group instructions?	☐	☐	☐
10. Begin to show an understanding of moral standards: right from wrong, fairness, honesty, good from bad?	☐	☐	☐

Developmental Checklist, continued

Does the child . . .	Yes	No	Sometimes
11. Look forward to, and enjoy, school?	☐	☐	☐
12. Appear to hear well and listen attentively?	☐	☐	☐
13. Enjoy reasonably good health, with few episodes of illness or health-related complaints?	☐	☐	☐
14. Have a good appetite and enjoy mealtimes?	☐	☐	☐
15. Take care of own personal hygiene without assistance?	☐	☐	☐
16. Sleep through the night, waking up refreshed and energetic?	☐	☐	☐

DEVELOPMENTAL ALERTS

Check with a health care provider or early childhood specialist if, by the *eleventh* birthday, the child *does not*:

- Continue to grow at a rate appropriate for the child's gender.
- Show continued improvement of fine motor skills.
- Make or keep friends.

Child's Name _____   Age _____

Observer _____   Date _____

Developmental Checklist (by 12 and 13 years)

Does the child . . .	Yes	No	Sometimes
1. Appear to be growing: increasing height and maintaining a healthy weight (not too thin or too heavy)?	☐	☐	☐
2. Understand changes associated with puberty or have an opportunity to learn and ask questions?	☐	☐	☐
3. Complain of headaches or blurred vision?	☐	☐	☐
4. Have an abnormal posture or curving of the spine?	☐	☐	☐
5. Seem energetic and not chronically fatigued?	☐	☐	☐
6. Stay focused on a task and complete assignments?	☐	☐	☐
7. Remember and carry out complex instructions?	☐	☐	☐
8. Sequence, order, and classify objects?	☐	☐	☐
9. Use longer and more complex sentence structure?	☐	☐	☐
10. Engage in conversation; tell jokes and riddles?	☐	☐	☐
11. Enjoy playing organized games and team sports?	☐	☐	☐

Developmental Checklist, continued Does the child ...	Yes	No	Sometimes
12. Respond to anger-invoking situations without resorting to violence or physical aggression?	☐	☐	☐
13. Begin to understand and solve complex mathematical problems?	☐	☐	☐
14. Accept blame for actions on most occasions?	☐	☐	☐
15. Enjoy competition?	☐	☐	☐
16. Accept and carry out responsibility in a dependable manner?	☐	☐	☐
17. Go to bed willingly and wake up refreshed?	☐	☐	☐
18. Take pride in appearance; keep self reasonably clean?	☐	☐	☐

- Enjoy going to school and show interest in learning (have children's hearing and vision tested; vision and hearing problems affect children's ability to learn and their interest in learning).

- Approach new situations with reasonable confidence.

- Handle failure and frustration in a constructive manner.

- Sleep through the night or *does* experience prolonged problems with bedwetting, nightmares, or sleepwalking.

DEVELOPMENTAL ALERTS

Check with a health care provider or early childhood specialist if, by the *thirteenth* birthday, the child *does not*:

- Have movements that are smooth and coordinated.

- Have energy sufficient for playing, riding bikes, or engaging in other desired activities.

- Stay focused on tasks at hand.

- Understand basic cause-and-effect relationships.

- Handle criticism and frustration with a reasonable response (physical aggression and excessive crying could be an indication of other underlying problems).

- Exhibit a healthy appetite (frequent skipping of meals is not typical for this age group).

- Make and keep friends.

Some content in this section is adapted from Allen, E. A. and Marotz, L., *Developmental Profiles: Pre-birth through Twelve* (4th ed.), published by Thomson Delmar Learning.

DEVELOPMENTAL MILESTONES BY SKILL

As with the list of milestones by age, this list is not exhaustive, but it can be used to arrange an environment or to plan activities in your room.

FIVE-YEAR-OLDS

Physical	Date Observed
Walks backward, heel to toe	
Walks unassisted up and down stairs, alternating feet	
Learns to turn somersaults (should be taught the right way in order to avoid injury)	
Touches toes without flexing knees	
Catches a ball thrown from three feet away	
Rides a tricycle or wheeled toy with speed and skillful steering; some learn to ride bicycles, usually with training wheels	
Cognitive	
Forms rectangle from two triangular cuts	
Builds steps with set of small blocks	
Understands concept of same shape, same size	
Sorts objects on the basis of two dimensions, such as color and form	
Sorts objects so that all things in the group have a single common feature	
Understands smallest and shortest; places objects in order from shortest to tallest, smallest to largest	
Language	
Has vocabulary of 1,500 words or more	
Tells a familiar story while looking at pictures in a book	
Uses functional definitions: a ball is to bounce; a bed is to sleep in	

Language, continued	Date Observed
Identifies and names four to eight colors	
Recognizes the humor in simple jokes; makes up jokes and riddles	
Produces sentences with five to seven words; much longer sentences are not unusual	
Social/Emotional	
Enjoys friendships; often has one or two special playmates	
Shares toys, takes turns, plays cooperatively (with occasional lapses); is often quite generous	
Participates in play and activities with other children; suggests imaginative and elaborate play ideas	
Is affectionate and caring, especially toward younger or injured children and animals	
Follows directions and carries out assignments usually; generally does what parent or teacher requests	
Continues to need adult comfort and reassurance, but may be less open in seeking and accepting comfort	

SIX-YEAR-OLDS

Physical	Date Observed
Has increased muscle strength; typically boys are stronger than girls of similar size	
Gains greater control over large and fine motor skills; movements are more precise and deliberate although some clumsiness persists	
Enjoys vigorous physical activity: running, jumping, climbing, and throwing	
Moves constantly, even when trying to sit still	
Has increased dexterity, eye–hand coordination, and improved motor functioning, which facilitate learning to ride a bicycle, swim, swing a bat, or kick a ball	
Enjoys art projects: likes to paint, model with clay, "make things," draw and color, work with wood	
Cognitive	
Shows increased attention; works at tasks for longer periods, although concentrated effort is not always consistent	
Understands simple time markers (today, tomorrow, yesterday) or uncomplicated concepts of motion (cars go faster than bicycles)	

Cognitive, continued	Date Observed
Recognizes seasons and major holidays and the activities associated with each	
Enjoys puzzles, counting and sorting activities, paper-and-pencil mazes, and games that involve matching letters and words with pictures	
Recognizes some words by sight; attempts to sound out words (some may read well by this time)	
Identifies familiar coins: pennies, nickels, dimes, quarters	
Language	
Loves to talk, often nonstop; may be described as a chatterbox	
Carries on adult-like conversations; asks many questions	
Learns five to ten new words daily; vocabulary consists of 10,000 to 14,000 words	
Uses appropriate verb tenses, word order, and sentence structure	
Uses language (not tantrums or physical aggression) to express displeasure: "That's mine! Give it back, you dummy."	
Talks self through steps required in simple problem-solving situations (although the "logic" may be unclear to adults)	
Social/Emotional	
Experiences mood swings: "best friends" then "worst enemies;" loving then uncooperative and irritable; especially unpredictable toward mother or primary caregiver	
Becomes less dependent on parents as friendship circle expands; still needs closeness and nurturing but has urges to break away and "grow up"	
Needs and seeks adult approval, reassurance, and praise; may complain excessively about minor hurts to gain more attention	
Continues to be egocentric; still sees events almost entirely from own perspective: views everything and everyone as there for own benefit	
Easily disappointed and frustrated by self-perceived failure	
Has difficulty composing and soothing self; cannot tolerate being corrected or losing at games; may sulk, cry, refuse to play, or reinvent rules to suit own purposes	

SEVEN-YEAR-OLDS

Physical	Date Observed
Exhibits large and fine motor control that is more finely tuned	
Tends to be cautious in undertaking more challenging physical activities, such as climbing up or jumping down from high places	

Physical, continued	Date Observed
Practices a new motor skill repeatedly until mastered then moves on to something else	
Finds floor more comfortable than furniture when reading or watching television; legs often in constant motion	
Uses knife and fork appropriately, but inconsistently	
Tightly grasps pencil near the tip; rests head on forearm, lowers head almost to the table top when doing pencil-and-paper tasks	
Cognitive	
Understands concepts of space and time in both logical and practical ways: a year is "a long time"; 100 miles is "far away"	
Begins to grasp Piaget's concepts of conservation (the shape of a container does not necessarily reflect what it can hold)	
Gains a better understanding of cause and effect: "If I'm late for school again, I'll be in big trouble."	
Tells time by the clock and understands calendar time—days, months, years, seasons	
Plans ahead: "I'm saving this cookie for tonight."	
Shows marked fascination with magic tricks; enjoys putting on "shows" for parents and friends	
Language	
Enjoys storytelling; likes to write short stories, tell imaginative tales	
Uses adult-like sentence structure and language in conversation; patterns reflect cultural and geographical differences	
Becomes more precise and elaborate in use of language; greater use of descriptive adjectives and adverbs	
Uses gestures to illustrate conversations	
Criticizes own performance: "I didn't draw that right," "Her picture is better than mine."	
Verbal exaggerations are commonplace: "I ate ten hot dogs at the picnic."	
Social/Emotional	
Is cooperative and affectionate toward adults and less frequently annoyed with them; sees humor in everyday happenings	
Likes to be the "teacher's helper"; eager for teacher's attention and approval but less obvious about seeking it	
Seeks out friendships; friends are important, but can stay busy if no one is available	

Social/Emotional, continued	Date Observed
Quarrels less often, although squabbles and tattling continue in both one-on-one and group play	
Complains that family decisions are unjust, that a particular sibling gets to do more or is given more	
Blames others for own mistakes; makes up alibis for personal shortcomings: "I could have made a better one, but my teacher didn't give me enough time."	

EIGHT-YEAR-OLDS

Physical	Date Observed
Enjoys vigorous activity; likes to dance, roller blade, swim, wrestle, bicycle, fly kites	
Seeks opportunities to participate in team activities and games: soccer, baseball, kickball	
Exhibits significant improvement in agility, balance, speed, and strength	
Copies words and numbers from blackboard with increasing speed and accuracy; has good eye–hand coordination	
Possesses seemingly endless energy	
Cognitive	
Collects objects; organizes and displays items according to more complex systems; bargains and trades with friends to obtain additional pieces	
Saves money for small purchases; eagerly develops plans to earn cash for odd jobs; studies catalogs and magazines for items to purchase	
Begins taking an interest in what others think and do; understands there are differences of opinion, cultures, distant countries	
Accepts challenge and responsibility with enthusiasm; delights in being asked to perform tasks at home and in school; interested in being rewarded	
Likes to read and work independently; spends considerable time planning and making lists	
Understands perspective (shadow, distance, shape); drawings reflect more realistic portrayal of objects	
Language	
Delights in telling jokes and riddles	
Understands and carries out multiple-step instructions (up to five steps); may need directions repeated because of not listening to the entire request	

Language, continued	Date Observed
Enjoys writing letters or sending e-mail messages to friends; includes imaginative and detailed descriptions	
Uses language to criticize and compliment others; repeats slang and curse words	
Understands and follows rules of grammar in conversation and written form	
Is intrigued with learning secret word codes and using code language	
Converses fluently with adults; can think and talk about past and future: "What time are we leaving to get to the swim meet next week?"	
Social/Emotional	
Begins forming opinions about moral values and attitudes; declares things right or wrong	
Plays with two or three "best" friends, most often the same age and gender; also enjoys spending some time alone	
Seems less critical of own performance but is easily frustrated when unable to complete a task or when the product does not meet expectations	
Enjoys team games and activities; values group membership and acceptance by peers	
Continues to blame others or makes up alibis to explain own shortcomings or mistakes	
Enjoys talking on the telephone with friends	

9- TO 13-YEAR-OLDS

Cognitive	Date Observed
Is capable of sustained interest	
Begins to think logically	
Begins to understand cause and effect	
Understands abstract concepts	
Applies logic and solves problems	
Considers more than one solution to problems	
Enjoys problem-solving games and puzzles	
Language	
Uses language to communicate ideas	
Uses language to express feelings	

Language, continued	Date Observed
Uses abstract words	
Often resorts to slang and profanity	
Is often argumentative and contradicts adults	
Social/Emotional	
Is sensitive to criticism	
Looks for friendly relationships with adults	
Makes value judgments about their own behavior	
Is aware of the importance of belonging	
Exhibits strong conformation to gender role	
Is independent and self-sufficient	
Begins to develop a moral values system	
May experience stress due to physical changes	
Seeks self-identity	
Physical	
Has high energy level	
Girls begin adolescent growth spurt	
Boys follow with a growth spurt	
Early maturing is related to positive self-image	
Boys have improved motor development and coordination	
Both boys and girls master skills necessary for playing games	

Some content in this section is adapted from Allen, E. A. and Marotz, L., *Developmental Profiles: Pre-birth through Twelve* (4th ed.), published by Thomson Delmar Learning.

PLAY MATERIALS FOR CHILDREN

Children construct their own understanding of the world around them as they interact with appropriate materials and with other people. Teachers play an important role in providing choices of good quality playthings that match children's developmental abilities and interests. When budgets are limited, it is vital for teachers to be able to select toys and materials that will provide optimum learning opportunities. Creative teachers learn how to "scrounge" for toys, and to make playthings out of recycled materials.

The lists that follow suggest the materials that are priorities for children at particular levels of development.

FOR CHILDREN OVER AGE FIVE

For gross motor play

- small wagons and wheelbarrows
- replications of adult tools for pushing and pretend play, such as lawn mower, shopping cart
- scooters
- tricycles and other vehicles with steering ability
- riding toys for more than one child
- balls of all sizes, especially 10–12 inch balls for kicking and throwing
- hollow plastic bat and lightweight ball
- jump rope
- stationary outdoor climbing equipment

- slides and ladders

- outdoor building materials, tires, and other loose parts

Exploration and mastery play materials

- sand and water play: measures, funnels, tubes, sand tools

- construction materials: unit blocks, large hollow blocks

- Legos®-type plastic interlocking blocks

- puzzles, including fit-in puzzles and large, simple jigsaw puzzles, with varying numbers of pieces, according to children's age

- pattern-making materials: beads for stringing, pegboards, mosaic boards, feltboards, color cubes

- dressing, lacing, and stringing: sewing cards and dressing frames

- collections of small plastic objects for matching, sorting, and ordering, by color, shape, size, or other category concepts

- simple, concrete number materials for counting and matching to numerals

- measuring materials: scales, measuring cups for liquids

- science materials: magnifying glass, color paddles, objects from the natural world, including pets

- beginning computer programs

- games: dominoes, lotto games, bingo by color, number, or picture, first board games that use concepts such as color or counting, Memory

- books of all kinds: picture books, realistic stories, alphabet picture books, poetry, information books

- writing center materials: clipboards, colored pencils, old calendars, envelopes, notepads, stationery, rubber stamps and ink pads, rulers, magnetic letters, stencil shapes, stickers, file cards and office materials

For pretend play

- dolls of various ethnic and gender appearance, with clothes and other accessories and furniture

- housekeeping equipment

- variety of dress-ups, including those related to various roles and themes

- transportation toys

- hand puppets

- animal and human figures for play scenes

- full length, unbreakable mirror

For creative play

- art and craft materials: crayons, markers, easel, paintbrushes, paint and finger-paint, varieties of paper, chalkboard and chalk, safety scissors, glue, collage materials, clay and playdough, and tools to use with them

- workbench with hammer, saw, and nails

- musical instruments

- recorded music for singing, movement and dancing, listening, and for using with rhythm instruments

FOR CHILDREN SIX THROUGH EIGHT YEARS

For gross motor play

- balls and sports equipment for beginning team play, such as soccer, baseball

- complex climbing structures: ropes, ladders, rings, hanging bars

- materials for target practice

- mats for acrobatics

- bicycles and scooters

For exploration and mastery play

- construction materials for large constructions and for creating models, including metal parts and nuts and bolts

- puzzles: 100-piece jigsaw puzzles, three-dimensional puzzles like Rubik's cubes

- craft materials for braiding, weaving, knitting, leather craft, jewelry making, sewing

- pattern-making materials: mosaic tiles, geometric puzzles

- games: word games, simple card games, reading and spelling games, number and counting games, beginning strategy games such as checkers

- materials for specific learning: printing materials, math manipulatives, measuring materials, science materials, and computer programs for language arts, number and concept development, and for problem-solving activities

- books at a variety of levels for beginning readers—see the Resources list in the supplement

For creative activities

- variety of markers, colored pencils, chalks, paintbrushes and paints, art papers for tracing and drawing

- clay and tools, including pottery wheel

- workbench with wood and variety of tools

- real instruments such as guitars and recorders

- music for singing and movement

- audiovisual materials for independent use

Some ideas adapted from *The Right Stuff for Children Birth to 8: Selecting play materials to support development.* M. Bronson. Washington, DC: NAEYC, 1995.

BEAUTIFUL JUNK LIST

Remember that recycled materials and other loose parts have many uses for exploration and creativity.

The following materials can be valuable instructional tools in the art program as well as in other curriculum areas.

- Empty plastic containers—detergent bottles, bleach bottles, old refrigerator containers. These can be used for constructing scoops, storing art materials, etc.

- Buttons—all colors and sizes. These are excellent for collages, assemblages, as well as sorting, counting, matching, etc.

- Egg shells. These can be washed, dried, and colored with food coloring for art projects.

- Coffee or shortening can lids and cans themselves. These can be covered with adhesive paper and used for the storage of art supplies, games, and manipulative materials.

- Magazines with colorful pictures. These are excellent for making collages, murals, and posters.

- Scraps of fabric—felt, silk, cotton, oil cloth, etc. These can be used to make "fabric boards" with the name of each fabric written under a small swatch attached to the board, as well as for collages, puppets, etc.

- Yarn scraps. These can be used for separating buttons into sets; also for art activities.

- Styrofoam scraps.

- Scraps of lace, rick rack, or decorative trim.

- Bottles with sprinkler tops. Excellent for water play and for mixing water as children fingerpaint.

- Wallpaper books of discontinued patterns.

- Paper doilies.

- Discarded wrapping paper.

- Paint color cards from paint/hardware stores.

- Old paintbrushes.

- Old jewelry and beads.

- Old muffin tins. These are effective for sorting small objects and mixing paint.

- Tongue depressors or ice cream sticks. Counters for math, good for art construction projects, stick puppets, etc.

- Wooden clothespins. For making "people," for construction projects, for hanging up paintings to dry.

Adapted from Mayesky, M., *Creative Activities for Young Children*, (7th ed.), published by Thomson Delmar Learning.

OBSERVATION AND ASSESSMENT

There are a variety of tools that can be used to assess children's development. Using assessment tools in conjunction with developmental milestones helps caregivers recognize a child's developmental accomplishments as well as determine the child's next growth steps. Not all children will give as much time to the teacher's directions. The teacher needs to observe each child to determine the level to which each child is performing independently so that instruction can begin. This knowledge is useful in planning curriculum, designing the room environment for success, and in establishing appropriate techniques that help children manage their own behavior. No doubt your college practicum experience taught you the logistics of observing: using objective descriptions and recording specific, dated, brief, and factual information. Observation can take many forms:

- anecdotal records

- running records

- checklists

- time or event sampling.

ANECDOTAL RECORDS

Anecdotal records are brief notes kept by the teacher while the child is performing a task. At first this may seem daunting, but it will become part of your everyday routine. Keep a small spiral notebook and pen or pencil in your pocket. When a child begins an activity, watch what the child does and write down three to four things that you actually observe the child doing. Remember the facts and only the facts. For example:

Johnny sits down at the science table. He has chosen a place where there are several different magnets and assorted objects. He picks up the largest magnet and puts it close to some of the objects. The objects jump up to meet the magnet. He laughs loudly and turns to show his friend sitting next to him.

As time permits, probably at the end of the school day, the brief notes are turned into a full scenario so that anyone could read the record at a later date.

ANECDOTAL RECORD

Child's Name: Johnny H.   Age: 7 yr. 5 mo.

Observer's Name: Jorge   Date: April 27, 2005

What actually happened/What I saw	Developmental Interpretation (Select one or two of the following)	
Johnny proudly shows his mom the painting he did today. He points out the colors he used and how he worked out a design. Johnny always greets the adults by their names when he arrives in the afternoon and sometimes even asks how they are today. He is polite when he has a request to make, usually remembering to say "please."	Interest in learning	
	Self-esteem/self-concept	X
	Cultural acceptance	
	Problem-solving	
	Interest in real life mathematical concepts	
	Interactions with adults	X
	Literacy	
	Interactions with peers	
	Language expression/comprehension	
	Self-regulation	
	Safe/healthy behavior	
	Self-help skills	
	Gross motor skills	
	Fine motor skills	X

ANECDOTAL RECORD

Child's Name: Date:

Observer's Name:

What actually happened/What I saw	Developmental Interpretation (Select one or two of the following)	
	Interest in learning	
	Self-esteem/self-concept	
	Cultural acceptance	
	Problem-solving	
	Interest in real life mathematical concepts	
	Interactions with adults	
	Literacy	
	Interactions with peers	
	Language expression/comprehension	
	Self-regulation	
	Safe/healthy behavior	
	Self-help skills	
	Gross motor skills	
	Fine motor skills	

RUNNING RECORDS

Another form of authentic assessment is the running record. It covers a longer time span and gives more information than an anecdotal record. Often it may have a specific developmental focus such as "social interactions." A running record will give you information about other developmental areas because of its very detailed nature. This form of observation requires the caregiver to not be involved with children for several minutes while writing the observation. You will be setting yourself apart from the children and writing continuously, in as much detail as possible. You will write what the child does and says, by herself and in interactions with other people and materials. Use objective phrases and avoid interpretative and judgmental language. Note that the format for this form of assessment has two columns. The left column is for writing the actual observations and the right column is for connecting the observations to aspects of development. Remember to date all observations so you can notice developmental change over time.

RUNNING RECORD

Child's Name: Trish H.   Age: 7 yr. 5 mo.
Observer's Name: Jorge   Date: April 27, 2005

Developmental Focus: Social interactions with peers

• Trish, Tina, Christa, and Ramona were jumping rope in the play yard. Tina was jumping and Christa and Ramona were turning the rope. Trish watched.	Participates in cooperative activities
• Trish chanted the jump rope rhymes with Tina, "Teddy bear, teddy bear, turn around . . ."	Early literacy/expressive language
• Tina's foot caught on the rope and she stumbled to the ground. Trish immediately ran to her as Tina yelled at the other girls for turning the rope too fast. Trish said, "Tina are you OK? Is your knee hurt?"	Expresses empathy
• Trish continued, "My mom told me that when I trip I have to keep practicing and that someday my feet will learn how to move the way the rope does." Trish showed Tina the bandage on her knee.	Communicates knowledge of growing skills
• Trish helped Tina to her feet and said, "It's my turn now." Tina replied, "I didn't finish my turn yet." Trish moved away from the rope and stood in the waiting position. She had a frown on her face and said nothing else.	Self-regulation/controls emotions
• Tina repeated her jump rope rhyme. Trish did not chime in with saying the rhyme.	
• When Tina was finished. Trish loudly announced, "Now it is my turn!" She quickly stepped toward the rope.	Stands up for own rights
• Trish told the girls turning the rope to be careful turning because she still had a sore on her knee from the day before when she fell. "I don't want to hurt my knee again."	Asks for what she needs
• Trish said, "I want to jump to 75." The girls turned the rope, Trish started jumping and counting. She counted from 1 to 56 but stopped when her foot got caught on the rope. She turned to the other girls and said, "That's OK. I am still practicing." She stepped away from the rope.	Gross motor skills Math skill Self-awareness

CHECKLIST

A checklist is often used as a means of assessment because it is one of the easiest assessment tools to use. A checklist consists of a predetermined list of clearly observable developmental criteria for which the observer indicates "yes" or "no." The observer reads the developmental criteria and makes a checkmark if the decision is a "yes." This form of assessment requires that no additional notes be recorded. Many teachers design their own checklists to fit the specific needs of their program. The following checklist is an example of one that might be used to assess social skills of children.

SOCIAL SKILLS CHECKLIST

Child's Name: Age: yr. mo.
Observer's Name:

Skills	Dates
• Desires and can work near other children	
• Interacts with other children	
• Takes turns with other children	
• Enters play with others in positive manner	
• Shares materials and supplies	
• Stands up for own rights in positive manner	
• Forms friendships with peers	
• Engages in positive commentary on other children's work	
• Shows empathy	
• Negotiates/compromises with other children	
• Demonstrates pro-social behavior	
• Participates in cooperative group activities	
• Resolves conflicts with adult prompts	
• Resolves conflicts without adult prompts	

Make checklists for each center in your classroom and hang them on clipboards. When you observe the children at play in each center, check off skills by placing a date in the appropriate box.

TIME OR EVENT SAMPLING

The last type of observation that a teacher should perform is a time or event sampling. These are similar in focus, but different, too. A **time sampling** asks the teacher to set a timer and each time the timer goes off, the teacher looks at a particular child and writes down what the child is doing. Again only the facts are written:

The timer is set to go off every 10 minutes. I will look at Johnny and see what he is doing when I hear the timer. The timer goes off, I look at Johnny, 9:30 a.m. He is at the block corner, building a freeway labyrinth complete with several cars. The timer goes off again, 9:45 a.m. He is still in the block corner and Kevin has joined him.

As mentioned, an **event sampling** is similar, only the teacher looks at events instead of being directed by a timer. The teacher zeros in on an event and writes down all things that she sees pertaining to the event.

EVENT SAMPLE		
Antecedent	**Behavior**	**Consequence**
What happened before the child exhibited the behavior? (This is a clue to the cause of the behavior.)	What did the child do? (Hit someone, throw something, withdraw, etc.)	What happened as a result of the exhibited behavior?
Jessie and Kevin are building a structure together in the block area. Timmy walked up to Kevin and said, "Let's build a castle!" Kevin said, "No, I'm playing with Jessie. You can't play."	Timmy walked by the blocks, swung his leg and kicked down the blocks.	Kevin yelled at Timmy, "That was mine! You can't knock it down." Kevin cried. A teacher intervened by helping the boys resolve the conflict. Timmy helped rebuild the structure.

Assessment and observation may seem overwhelming as you begin your career in Early Childhood. Do not shy away from it. Take the challenge and begin to look for the positive aspects of learning and mastering a new skill. Picture yourself as a student in your classroom and imagine what it is like to perfect something your teacher has just asked you to do. How does it make you feel? Now begin.

- You have the day planned for outdoor activities and there is an unexpected rainstorm. What will you do?

- It is your day off and you get a call at the last minute to cover for a co-worker who is ill. You find out that nothing has been planned. What activities can you implement quickly?

- You were promised that the materials you needed for your planned art activity would be on site when you arrived at work, but there was a shipping delay and they are not there. What is an alternative activity you can easily set up and implement?

Being prepared at all times with a few back-up activities will make your job much less stressful. Some of the activities listed here require only a few materials that you might want to have on hand at all times.

CURRICULUM AREA: ART

Providing children with open-ended art activities allows them to be creative using their own ideas. This type of art also requires less adult supervision. Set-up time for the following activities should be minimal. Children can be involved in the set-up and clean-up processes.

Painting with disabilities
Developmental Focus: Physical

Goal: Children will experience painting as if they were disabled and unable to use their hands and arms

Age Range: Five and up

Materials: Paper, small paintbrushes, at least three colors of paint, containers for paint

Procedure: Engage the children in a discussion about people with disabilities. Encourage them to think of how people use their bodies differently to do things they want to do. For example: Some people use wheelchairs to help them move around. Others may use special equipment to help them reach things from high shelves. Some people have only one arm or do not have use of their hands. Lead children to thinking about how they could paint if they could not use their arms. Most likely they will think of foot or mouth painting. Invite them to participate in mouth painting. Provide paper, small paintbrushes and cups of paint. Remember that each child needs his or her own brush and it must be sanitized before another child may use it. If corks are available, they can be pushed onto the end of the paintbrush giving something larger for children to grip with their teeth. Extend the activity by inviting children to research foot and mouth artists on the Internet.

Puppets

Developmental Focus: Cognitive, Physical, Language Development

Goal: Children will use their creative skills to make paper bag puppets

Age Range: Five and up

Materials: Lunch paper bags, paper plates, tongue depressors, glue, scraps of paper, and yarn

Procedure: Encourage children to design their own puppets using their personal ideas. Do not give children a model to follow. Keep the bottom of the bag folded and place your hand inside the bag and over the fold to create the moving mouth of the puppet. Tongue depressors can be glued onto a paper plate to create another kind of puppet. You may want to begin the activity with a discussion about creating a puppet show. Involve children in writing a script so they can later perform with their puppets. Encourage them to act out a favorite story. This activity works well with small teams of children as well as with individual children.

Fold painting

Developmental Focus: Physical

Goal: Children will experience mirrored images created from paper that is painted and folded

Age Range: Four and up

Materials: Paper, paintbrushes, paint, newspapers

Procedure: Provide children with a piece of paper, paintbrushes, and a few colors of paint. Instruct children to fold the paper in half and paint only one half of the paper. When they are ready they can fold the paper in half. Rub the outside of the paper. When opened it will make a perfectly mirrored design. If the paper has a lot of paint on it, encourage the child to place it inside a sheet of newspaper before rubbing the outside of it, allowing any excess paint to be squished onto the newspaper instead of the work surface.

Spiral snakes

Developmental Focus: Physical

Goal: Children will create a curved snake made from a paper spiral

Age Range: Five and up

Materials: Square piece of paper, scissors, crayons or markers

Procedure: Demonstrate how to make spirals on a piece of paper. Younger children may need to have you make the spirals. Start in the middle of the paper and draw a spiral. Keep the lines of the spiral about one to one-and-a-half inches apart. The spiral can then be colored and cut out.

Draw a funny creature

Developmental Focus: Social, Physical, Language and Communication

Goal: Children will work collaboratively in teams to draw creatures

Age Range: Six and up

Materials: 8.5″ × 11″ paper and pencils for each child

Procedure: Each child is given a piece of paper to be folded in half from top to bottom. The children work in teams of two. One person will draw the top half of a creature on the top of his page. Instruct the children to have the center of the fold be the center of the creature's body. The other child will draw on his own paper the bottom half of a person using the center of the fold for the center of the body. Each child will then flip their paper over so the blank side of the paper is facing up. They will switch papers. Without looking at the other person's drawings, the children will switch papers and again draw another creature's top of bottom body parts. Once completed the papers can be unfolded to view the creatures created by their teamwork. Extend the activity by providing crayons for coloring the creatures.

Add your own art activity ideas

_____

_____

_____

_____

_____

_____

_____

_____

_____

_____

CURRICULUM AREA: SCIENCE

Like art, science activities can also be open-ended. Science activities that give children materials to discover physics concepts can provide hours of enjoyment as well as an opportunity to learn. The following activities involve movement. The set-up time for these activities will be minimal if the materials are readily available within the classroom.

Rollways

Developmental Focus: Physical, Cognitive

Goal: Household materials will be used to create a structure for rolling marbles

Age Range: Four and up

Materials: Marbles, paper towel and toilet paper tubes, paper cups, berry baskets, dry sponges or small blocks

Procedure: Encourage children to build their own marble maze. Suggest that the children look around the room for other items that can be used to build their maze. The maze can be free-standing on a table or can be more permanently affixed to a large piece of cardboard. Use blocks or other objects and place them around the edge of the table to prevent marbles from rolling onto the floor.

Water movers

Developmental Focus: Cognitive, Physical

Goal: Children will use various objects to explore movement of water

Age Range: Three and up

Materials: Vinyl tubing, funnels, basting bulbs, plastic containers, large containers, water, small buckets, towels for clean-up

Procedure: Vinyl tubing can be purchased at most hardware stores. Look for a diameter into which the end of a funnel can easily fit. Have a variety of lengths of tubing—from one foot to four feet. Ask children to think about how they can move water from one container to another by using the materials provided. Build some of the children's ideas.

Tree exploration

Developmental Focus: Cognitive, Social, Physical, Language and Communication

Goal: Children will work in teams of three to examine a tree

Age Range: Five and up

Materials: Paper and old crayons, pencils, paper bags, easel paper, glue

Procedure: Invite children to discuss the various parts of trees before beginning the exploration. Children will then take their team to a nearby tree to examine it. Encourage children to close their eyes and feel the bark. A child can make a rubbing by rolling the side of the crayon over a piece of paper on the tree trunk. Another child can make a rubbing of a tree leaf. The third child can examine the tree roots and draw their profile on paper. All three children can work together examining the ground under the tree to gather things that may have fallen from the tree. These things can be placed in the bag for further use in the classroom. The children can examine the tree to see if there is a nest in it or if there are any insects on the trunk. Encourage children to notice the difference in the leaves. Notice their size, shape, and color. Once the children are in the classroom, they can work together to create a display of their tree investigation on a piece of easel paper. Extend the activity by examining different kinds of trees, including pine trees, trees that are blooming, and trees that are barren.

Add your own science activity ideas

_____

_____

_____

_____

_____

_____

_____

_____

_____

_____

_____

_____

CURRICULUM AREA: INDOOR GAMES

There are many indoor games that do not require materials or special room arrangement. Part of the intrigue for children is the involvement of the caregiver. Children like playing with adults. One technique to manage indoor games is to use talking sticks. Write each child's name on a tongue depressor and keep it in a small can. When deciding whose turn it is, simply pull out a name.

20 questions

Developmental Focus: Cognitive, Language and Communication

Goal: Children will use their deductive reasoning skills to play this guessing game

Age Range: Five and up

Procedure: Begin the game by pretending that you are hiding somewhere in the room and that you are any size you want to be. Children take turns asking questions to try to guess where you are hiding. All questions must be asked in such a way that they require only a yes or no answer. Initially children will simply make guesses such as, "Are you on the bookcase?" Teach children to develop deductive thinking skills by asking questions like, "Are you smaller than this block? Are you in the top half of the room? Are you touching something made of wood?" Children can ask a total of 20 questions to try and guess where you are. Invite a child to hide after modeling how to play the game a few times. Extend the game by pretending to be an object in the room and having the children guess what you are.

Word change

Developmental Focus: Cognitive, Social

Goal: Children will build on their listening and language skills to play a word game

Age Range: Five and up

Procedure: With children sitting in a circle, begin the game with a simple sentence. The object of the game is that each child will pass the sentence to the next child. One word in the sentence must be changed each time it is passed. For example, "The boy went to the school." The next child responds, "Oh! No, no! The policeman went to the school." The next child replies, "Oh! No, no!! The policeman went to the zoo." Encourage unusual combinations and do not worry if they do not make sense. Be sensitive to second-language learners as they may need more processing time to understand the game. Encourage them to include vocabulary from their language. You may need to set a time limit.

Indoor freeze tag

Developmental Focus: Physical, Cognitive

Goal: Children will play slow motion freeze tag until there is only one person left unfrozen

Age Range: Five and up

Procedure: Children can play slow tag inside the classroom by using slow movements. To begin, clear as much space as possible by moving tables and chairs to one side of the room. (If space is limited, you may decide to have half the class sit around the edge of the room to watch and the other half participate. Once a round of the game is complete, the children can switch places.) Demonstrate exaggerated, slow movements. To play, taggers "run" in slow motion trying to tag another person. When a person gets tagged, he or she must stay frozen in that position. Play continues until only one person is left unfrozen. Encourage the children who are watching to observe the techniques they can use when it is their turn to play.

Transformer

Developmental Focus: Physical, Cognitive, Language and Communication

Goal: Children will pretend being a variety of animals as directed by a person chosen to be the transformer. They will work together to hide the identity of the transformer

Age Range: Five and up

Procedure: Have the children stand in a circle with their eyes closed and hands behind their back. As leader of the group you will walk behind the group and select a child to be the transformer. On your signal, the children will begin to act like an animal of their choosing. As they act out their animal, they will be whispering to each other. The transformer will whisper to another player such things as "You are a dog." Slowly after a few moments, that child will begin to transform into a dog. He must protect the identity of the transformer. The transformer will continue transforming other children. Players will continue whispering to each other as if they were the transformer. The goal is for the children to guess the identity of the transformer. If a child suspects he knows the identity of the transformer, he will freeze in his position and loudly say, "I suspect!" All players will freeze. The child will continue by pointing to the suspected player saying, "You're a dog!" (or some other animal). If the person identified is the transformer, he immediately becomes the animal named. If not, the accuser becomes that animal and the game continues.

Add your own indoor game ideas

_____

_____

_____

_____

_____

_____

_____

_____

_____

_____

_____

_____

CURRICULUM AREA: OUTDOOR GAMES

Children need ample time to play outside, especially after a day of being inside in a school classroom. Outdoor games are an opportunity to build relationships. On occasion children will seem exceptionally restless. It may be after a day of intense testing or after days of having to be inside due to inclement weather. It is important for a caregiver to be able to implement outdoor group games whenever the children seem restless and lacking a direction for their energy. Keep in mind that children particularly enjoy it when you are playing the game too. You will be the game organizer, the supervisor, and, possibly, a player. Involve other caregivers when working in teams so every team has a caregiver as a part of their team. Remember to be aware of and respect children who may not want to play and may need a special invitation to play or serve as a helper. Be sensitive to mood changes in the group. A rule of thumb when playing games is to quit when the children are still emotionally excited about the game rather than when they are beginning to no longer want to play the game. If you quit when the children are on a high, they will want to play the game in the future. Always be aware of safety!

Ball pass

Developmental Focus: Physical, Social

Goal: Children will work together to quickly pass the balls from one person to another

Age Range: Five and up

Materials: Two or more large balls for each group

Procedure: A group of 8 to 10 children will stand in a circle to play this game. Too few children make the game hard to play and too many mean that children have to wait too long to play. Begin play by having one child pass the ball to the person next to him in whatever manner he chooses such as through the legs, over his head, etc. While passing the children chant in rhythm, "Pass the ball, pass the ball." The chanting helps to keep the ball moving at a faster pace. Once play is going, add a second ball to the group and have it move in the opposite direction. Occasionally, you may want to announce, "Switch!" and children will have to reverse the direction of passing the ball. Adding more balls keeps the game exciting. Watch the play of the children and their mood and signal stop when the game becomes a free-for-all.

Amoeba tag

Developmental Focus: Physical, Social

Goal: In this game of tag, the tagged children link with the taggers and work together until all children are tagged

Age Range: Five and up

Procedure: Select two people to be "it." One method for choosing children to start the game is by having children stand in a close circle with one arm outstretched and the hand in a fist. Beginning with a randomly selected fist, use "Eenie, meenie, minie, mo." As you chant, touch one child's outstretched fist each time you say a word. The child you touch when you say the word "one" will be "it." Repeat the procedure to select the second child. The two children who are "it" will hold hands and chase other children. When they touch another person, that person is considered tagged and must join the chain by linking hands. The three of them continue with hands linked to tag other children. When a fourth child is tagged, she must join the link. When a link of children is an even number of at least four children, it may split. The teams may link together at will. The game continues until all children are tagged and linked together.

Shadow tag

Developmental Focus: Physical, Cognitive, Social

Goal: A tagged child, chases other children's shadows trying to tag them and thereby make them "it"

Age Range: Five and up

Procedure: This form of tag is best played later in the afternoon when the shadows are longer. The child selected to be "it" tries to step on the shadow of another child. When a player gets tagged, she becomes the new "it." A variation of this is for children tagged to stand frozen in their tagged position. They are frozen until all children have been tagged. Then a new child is selected to be "it."

Dragon's tail

Developmental Focus: Physical, Social, Cognitive

Goal: The front of a line of children tries to catch the tail of the line

Age Range: Five and up

Procedure: All the children stand in line holding onto the waist of the child in front of them. The front player is the head and the last child is the tail. The head must try to catch the tail while keeping the dragon from breaking in two. Once the head has successfully touched the tail, the two people who played the head and the tail move to the middle of the dragon, creating a new head and tail. Set a time limit for each dragon to accomplish its goal. Occasionally the children may not be able to reach each other in the allotted time. This will give other children a chance to play the head and tail roles. Encourage the children to try different numbers of players in the dragon. Two or more dragons can play at once.

Add your own outdoor game ideas

_____

_____

_____   _____

_____

_____

_____

_____

_____

_____

_____

_____

_____

A number of Web sites offer sample lesson plans for teachers. When downloading lesson plans from the Internet or another source, be sure each plan includes:

- objective or goal of the lesson

- materials needed

- directions for the activity

- appropriate age group

- developmental appropriateness.

Check the resources section of this manual for a list of Web sites with lesson plans and other free materials for teachers.

BOOKS FOR CHILDREN

Reading aloud is a wonderful gift you can give to children. Through sharing an interesting book, you introduce them to a world they might not otherwise be able to visit. You can travel anywhere you like; you can have experiences that are outside the realm of your current environment; you can participate in wonderful fantasies; you can be saddened, then uplifted.

Children's desire to read and the ability to do so is fostered by being read to as soon as they are born. Even babies can enjoy looking at picture books and hearing simple stories. Preschoolers love to have favorite books read to them repeatedly. As children move into the school years, they can sustain their interest in longer books that are divided into chapters. When they realize the joy that comes from good books, they are more motivated to read on their own.

Many textbooks provide suggestions for setting up reading corners and providing books for children to read by themselves. This section will focus on books that you can read aloud to children in small or large groups. Remember that the more you read, the better you will become at doing so. When the books have been enjoyed in a group setting, add them to the book corner for children to read alone. In addition, teachers often create lending arrangements where children can take home books for their parents to read and then return. Teachers who believe in the importance of reading choose the best of children's literature and involve families in reading.

HOW TO GET CHILDREN TO LISTEN AND WANT MORE

- Schedule time each day for reading, maybe toward the end of the day when children are tired and will enjoy the inactivity; make sure the setting is comfortable.

- Choose books that you also enjoy, perhaps one you read as a child; preview the book before presenting it to the children in case there are passages you want to shorten.

- The first time you read a book, state the title and author. Research for interesting facts about the author to share with the children. If there is an illustrator, include that information as well.

- If you are reading to a large group, position yourself so that you are slightly higher than the children so that your voice will project more easily.

- If you are reading to a small group, sit among them in a more intimate placement, which will draw them to you and the book.

- Occasionally stop and ask, "What do you think is going to happen next?"

- Read at a pace that allows children to build mental images of the characters or setting; change your pace to match the action of the story: slow your pace and lower you voice during a suspenseful spot and then speed up when the action does.

- Allow time for discussion only if children wish to do so. Let them voice fears, ask questions, or share their thoughts about the book. Do not turn it into a quiz or need to interpret the story.

- Practice reading aloud, trying to vary your expression or tone of voice.

- Create a display of images or information pertaining to the book you are reading. A map will allow children to pinpoint places mentioned in the story. Pictures, charts, or time lines will also add to the display. Objects or foods mentioned in the book add another dimension.

- Find a stopping place each day that will create suspense, so that the children are eager to get back to the book the next day.

- When you pick up the book the next day, ask if they remember what had happened just before you stopped reading.

WHAT NOT TO DO

- Do not read a book you do not enjoy; your feelings will be sensed by the children.

- Do not read a book when it becomes obvious that it was a poor choice; previewing the book before presenting it to the children can minimize these kinds of mistakes.

- Do not choose a book with which some of the children are already familiar; they may have heard it at home or seen a version on television or the movies.

- Do not start a book unless you have enough time to read more than a few pages.

- Do not be fooled by awards. Just because a book has received a national book award does not mean that it is suitable for your particular group of children.

- Do not impose on the children your own interpretations or reactions to the story. Let them express their own understanding and feelings.

FINDING BOOKS

Internet sources for recommended books for children of all ages:

http://www.tchliteracy.com

http://www.kid-lit.com

http://www.bookitfamilies.com

http://www.carolhurst.com

http://www.read2kids.org

Book source
Trelease, J. (2001). *The read-aloud handbook* (5th ed.), New York: Penguin Group.

BOOK LIST

Aesop's Fables retold & illustrated by Charles Santore
Jell Press, 1988
All ages   48 pages
Twenty-four fables that contain wisdom and lessons to be learned.

Charlotte's Web by E.B. White; Garth Williams, Illustrator
Harper, 1952
Ages 5–9   184 pages
Charlotte, a gray spider, conspires with the farmer's daughter to save the life of a pig that is to be slaughtered in the fall. This book is beloved by both children and adults.

James and the Giant Peach by Roald Dahl
Knopf, 1961
Ages 5–12
Four-year-old James is sent to live with an abusive aunt who expects him to be a humble servant after the death of his parents. A giant peach grows in the back-yard, with a collection of characters inside, ready to capture James' imagination and make life easier for him.

Poppy by Avi
Orchard, 1995
Ages 5–9   160 pages
Poppy is a mouse who lives in Dimwood Forest where the mice population is kept under control by a fierce horned owl. When the owl kills Poppy's boyfriend, Poppy dares to venture into the world beyond Dimwood Forest. She eventually uncovers a hoax the owl has perpetuated over the years and moves her family to a better place.

The Story of Holly and Ivy by Rumer Godden; Barbara Cooney, Illustrator
Viking, 1985
Ages 5–10   31 pages
On Christmas Eve, a lonely runaway orphan girl dreams of a doll and a home.

Cam Jensen and the Mystery of the Dinosaur Bones by David Adler
Puffin, 1997
Ages 6–8   56 pages
On a visit to a museum, Cam notices that some of the dinosaur bones are missing. She sets out to solve the mystery. This is one of a series featuring Cam.

Chocolate Fever by Robert K. Smith
Dell, 1978
Ages 6–10   94 pages
Henry Green is a boy who absolutely loves chocolate and has some for every meal of the day. He is a prime candidate for a new disease "chocolate fever." Henry eventually has to learn about moderation.

The Chocolate Touch by Patrick S. Catling
Morrow, 1979
Ages 6–9   122 pages
Everything John touches turns to chocolate, from his morning toothpaste to his breakfast eggs. He wonders what would happen if he kisses his mother.

A Dog Called Kitty by Bill Wallace
Holiday, 1980
Ages 6–10   137 pages
A boy struggles to overcome his deep-seated fear of dogs caused by an encounter with a vicious dog when he was very young.

Herbie Jones by Suzy Kline
Putnam, 1985
Ages 6–9   95 pages
One of a series about Herbie and his friend Raymond. In this volume they get into a variety of escapades told with a lot of humor.

The Iron Giant: A Story in Five Nights by Ted Hughes
Harper, 1987
Ages 6–9   58 pages
This is a science fiction story about a robot without a master who roams the land eating up anything made of metal. (It has been made into a movie.) An alien creature lands on earth and the iron man is forced into a fight for his life.

Stone Fox by John R. Gardiner
Crowell, 1980
Ages 6–12   96 pages
Willy tries valiantly to save his beloved grandfather's farm by attempting to win the purse in a local bobsled race. Willy's efforts are helped by his loyal and determined dog.

Amber Brown is Not a Crayon by Paula Danziger
G.P. Putnam, 1994
Ages 7–9   80 pages
Amber and Justin are best friends. When they find that Justin will be moving, Amber is sad and knows everything is going to change.

The Bad Beginning by Lemony Snicket
Harper, 1999
Ages 7–9   162 pages
This is the first of a series by this popular author. Three orphans must overcome a series of misfortunes that are right out of a Dickens

novel. They do prevail over one villain after another, and are finally victorious.

Call it Courage by Armstrong Perry
Macmillan, 1940
Ages 7–12   94 pages
A young boy living in the South Seas struggles to overcome his fear of the ocean. He conquers that fear by eventually canoeing alone on the sea.

Homer Price by Robert McCloskey
Viking, 1943
Ages 7–10   160 pages
This is a collection of funny stories about a small-town boy and the dilemmas he faces, including foiling a bank robbery with his pet skunk.

Ida Early Comes Over the Mountain by Robert Burch
Viking, 1980
Ages 7–11   145 pages
Four motherless children finally have someone to care for them when Ida shows up at their house. Some have described Ida as the "Mary Poppins of the Blue Ridge Mountains."

The Monster's Ring by Bruce Coville
Pantheon, 1982
Ages 7–9   87 pages
This is a good story for Halloween celebrations. Timid Russell buys a ring that can turn him into a real monster that can vanquish a bully.

Mr. Popper's Penguins by Richard and Florence Atwater; Robert Lawson, Illustrator
Little, 1938
Ages 7–9   140 pages
When 12 penguins come to live with Mr. Hopper some unexpected problems arise.

The Secret Garden by Frances Hodgson Burnett
Numerous publishers
Ages 7–8   240 pages
Mary Lennox is shipped to England from India after her parents die of cholera. She goes to live in the huge house belonging to her Uncle Archibald Craven. While wandering through the immense mansion, she finds a secret garden that holds another secret.

The Lion, the Witch, and the Wardrobe by C.S. Lewis
HarperCollins, 1950
Ages 8–11
When they venture into an old wardrobe closet in an empty room, four children discover the magic kingdom of Narnia, where there are witches, princes, and lots of intrigue.

Peppermints in the Parlor by Barbara Brooks Wallace
Atheneum, 1980
Ages 8–12   198 pages
Emily, who has been newly orphaned, travels to San Francisco expecting to live with her wealthy aunt and uncle. Instead she finds the aunt held as a captive servant in a decaying home for the aged.

The Reluctant Dragon by Kenneth Grahame; Ernest H. Shepard, Illustrator
Holiday, 1938
Ages 8–10   54 pages
Greene is the author of the classic *Wind in the Willows*. Here he tells the story of a dragon that wants nothing to do with violence. A young boy knows a lot of dragon stories and wants to see a battle between the dragon and St. George, but also wants to protect his friend the dragon.

Skinnybones by Barbara Park
Knopf, 1982
Ages 8–10   112 pages
Alex Frankovich is a clumsy smart aleck who has to deal with losing ball games, sibling rivalry, and many other problems. He also throws tantrums, but is extremely funny when he does so.

Tales of a Fourth Grade Nothing by Judy Blume
Dutton, 1972
Ages 8–10   120 pages
Peter is in the fourth grade and has lots of problems caused by the antics of his younger sibling.

The Bear's House by Marilyn Sachs
Dutton, 1987
Ages 9–11   82 pages
A 10-year-old girl is taunted by her classmates because she sucks her thumb and wears dirty clothes. She retreats into a fantasy world.

Black Beauty by Anna Sewell; Charles Keeping, Illustrator
Farrar, 1990
Ages 9–12   214 pages
Set in the Victorian period, the book shows the cruelty to horses that existed at the time. The book, along with its illustrations, paints a vivid picture of life in that period.

The Friendship by Mildred Taylor
Dial, 1987
Ages 9 and up   53 pages
Set in rural Mississippi, this story portrays the cruelty of bigotry. Two men (one white, one black), once were friends, but have a falling out when the black man calls his friend by his first name. (There are some racial epithets in the book.)

From the Mixed-up Files of Mrs. Basil E. Frankweiller by E.L. Koningsburg
Macmillan, 1967
Ages 9–13   162 pages
Claudia convinces her younger brother to run away with her. They take refuge in New York's Metropolitan Museum of Art. They sleep, eat, and bathe in the midst of centuries-old art. They manage to hide from guards who are looking for them.

A Taste of Blackberries by Doris B. Smith
Crowell, 1973
Ages 9–12   52 pages
A boy tells of his best friend's death, which occurred when after he was stung by a bee. Readers share the child's deep sorrow and guilt about what happened.

The Wish Giver: Three Tales of Coven Tree by Bill Brittain
Harper, 1983
Ages 9–13   181 pages
A mysterious stranger arrives in the town of Coven Tree and sets up a tent at a church social. For 50 cents he says he can make wishes come true. Some of the townspeople find out that it would have been better if their wishes did not come true.

On My Honor by Marion Dane Bauer
Clarion, 1986
Ages 10–14   90 pages
Joel tells no one when his friend drowns accidentally. This is a story of choices since Joel denies the reality of the accident resulting in some difficult consequences.

Poetry

Honey, I Love by Eloise Greenfield; Diane and Leo Dillon, Illustrators
Ages Pre-school–8   42 pages
Sixteen short poems about things everybody loves.

Kids Pick the funniest Poems Compiled by Bruce Lansky; Stephen Carpenter, Illustrator
Meadowbrook, 1991
Ages 5–13   105 pages
Seventy-five funny poems chosen by 300 schoolchildren.

Never Take a Pig to Lunch and Other Poems About the Fun of Foods;
Selected and Illustrated by Nadine Bernard Westcot
Orchard, 1994
Ages 5–9   62 pages
Hilarious poems about food from four categories: silly things; foods we like; eating too much; manners.

Where The Sidewalk Ends by Shel Silverstein
Harper, 1974
Ages 5–13   166 pages
This collection contains 130 poems that all children will love.

DEVELOPMENTALLY APPROPRIATE PRACTICE

National Association for the Education of Young Children's (NAEYC) first position statement on Developmentally Appropriate Practice had two main motivations:

1. the process of accrediting centers required widely accepted and specific definitions of what constituted excellent practices in early childhood education

2. there was a proliferation of programs that had inappropriate practices and expectations for their children, largely based on premature academic learning.

The original position statement did enhance the early childhood profession, although it was not received with universal acceptance, so a revised position statement clarified some of the previous misunderstandings and expanded the vision of good practices.

It is important to keep the principles firmly in mind when making professional decisions. It is also important to use the statement in conversations with others regarding appropriate practices. Colleagues, administrators, and family members all have their individual understandings of what to do with young children. It is, therefore, useful for every teacher to have a copy of the position statement. In a conversation, you can use the position statement to replace the idea of personal opinions with the weight of the professional body of knowledge. The complete statement, *Developmentally Appropriate Practice in Early Childhood Programs*, Revised Edition (1997, NAEYC), is as follows:

DEVELOPMENTALLY APPROPRIATE PRACTICE IN EARLY CHILDHOOD PROGRAMS SERVING CHILDREN FROM BIRTH THROUGH AGE EIGHT

A Position Statement for the NAEYC Adopted July 1996.

This statement defines and describes principles of developmentally appropriate practice in early childhood programs for administrators, teachers, parents, policy-makers, and others who make decisions about the care and education of young children. An early childhood program is any group program in a center, school, or other facility that serves children from birth through age eight. Early childhood programs include child care centers, family child care homes, private and public preschools, kindergartens, and primary-grade schools.

The early childhood profession is responsible for establishing and promoting standards of high-quality professional practice in early childhood programs. These standards must reflect current knowledge and shared beliefs about what constitutes high-quality, developmentally appropriate early childhood education in the context within which services are delivered.

This position paper is organized into several components which include the following:

1. a description of the current context in which early childhood programs operate

2. a description of the rationale and need for NAEYC's position statement

3. a statement of NAEYC's commitment to children

4. the statement of the position and definition of *developmentally appropriate practice*

5. a summary of the principles of child development and learning and the theoretical perspectives that inform decisions about early childhood practice

6. guidelines for making decisions about developmentally appropriate practices that address the following integrated components of early childhood practice: creating a caring community of learners, teaching to enhance children's learning and development, constructing appropriate curriculum, assessing children's learning and development, and establishing reciprocal relationships with families

7. a challenge to the field to move from *either/or* to *both/and* thinking

8. recommendations for policies necessary to ensure developmentally appropriate practices for all children.

This statement is designed to be used in conjunction with NAEYC's "Criteria for High Quality Early Childhood Programs," the standards for accreditation by the National Academy of Early Childhood Programs (NAEYC 1991), and with "Guidelines for Appropriate Curriculum Content and Assessment in Programs Serving Children Ages 3 through 8" (NAEYC & NAECS/SDE 1992; Bredekamp & Rosegrant 1992, 1995).

The Current Context of Early Childhood Programs

The early childhood knowledge base has expanded considerably in recent years, affirming some of the profession's cherished beliefs about good practice and challenging others. In addition to gaining new knowledge, early childhood programs have experienced several important changes in recent years. The number of programs continues to increase not only in response to the growing demand for out-of-home child care but also in recognition of the critical importance of educational experiences during the early years (Willer et al. 1991; NCES 1993). For example, in the late 1980s Head Start embarked on the largest expansion in its history, continuing this expansion into the 1990s with significant new services for families with infants and toddlers. The National Education Goals Panel established as an objective of Goal 1 that by the year 2000 all children will have access to high-quality, developmentally appropriate preschool programs (NEGP 1991). Welfare reform portends a greatly increased demand for child care services for even the youngest children from very-low-income families.

Some characteristics of early childhood programs have also changed in recent years. Increasingly, programs serve children and families from diverse cultural and linguistic backgrounds, requiring that all programs demonstrate understanding of and responsiveness to cultural and linguistic diversity. Because culture and language are critical components of children's development, practices cannot be developmentally appropriate unless they are responsive to cultural and linguistic diversity.

The Americans with Disabilities Act and the Individuals with Disabilities Education Act now require that all early childhood programs make reasonable accommodations to provide access for children with disabilities or developmental delays (DEC/CEC & NAEYC 1993). This legal right reflects the growing consensus that young children with disabilities are best served in the same community settings where their typically developing peers are found (DEC/CEC 1994).

The trend toward full inclusion of children with disabilities must be reflected in descriptions of recommended practices, and considerable work has been done toward converging the perspectives of early childhood and early childhood special education (Carta et al. 1991; Mallory 1992, 1994; Wolery, Strain, & Bailey 1992; Bredekamp 1993b; DEC Task Force 1993; Mallory & New 1994b; Wolery & Wilbers 1994).

Other important program characteristics include age of children and length of program day. Children are now enrolled in programs at younger ages, many from infancy. The length of the program day for all ages of children has been extended in response to the need for extended hours of care for employed families. Similarly, program sponsorship has become more diverse. The public schools in the majority of states now provide prekindergarten programs, some for children as young as three, and many offer before- and after-school child care (Mitchell, Seligson, & Marx 1989; Seppanen, Kaplan deVries, & Seligson 1993; Adams & Sandfort 1994).

Corporate America has become a more visible sponsor of child care programs, with several key corporations leading the way in promoting high quality (for example, IBM, AT&T, and the American Business Collaboration). Family child care homes have become an increasingly visible sector of the child care community, with greater emphasis on professional development and the National Association for Family Child Care taking the lead in establishing an accreditation system for high-quality family child care (Hollestelle 1993; Cohen & Modigliani 1994; Galinsky et al. 1994). Many different settings in this country provide services to young children, and it is legitimate—even beneficial—for these settings to vary in certain ways. However, since it is vital to meet children's learning and developmental needs wherever they are served, high standards of quality should apply to all settings.

The context in which early childhood programs operate today is also characterized by ongoing debates about how best to teach young children and discussions about what sort of practice is most likely to contribute to their development and learning. Perhaps the most important contribution of NAEYC's 1987 position statement on developmentally appropriate practice (Bredekamp 1987) was that it created an opportunity for increased conversation within and outside the early childhood field about practices. In revising the position statement, NAEYC's goal is not only to improve the quality of current early childhood practice but also to continue to encourage the kind of questioning and debate among early childhood professionals that are necessary for the continued growth of professional knowledge in the field. A related goal is to express NAEYC's position more clearly so that energy is not wasted in unproductive debate about apparent rather than real differences of opinion.

Rationale for the Position Statement

The increased demand for early childhood education services is partly due to the increased recognition of the crucial importance of experiences during the earliest years of life. Children's experiences during early childhood not only influence their later functioning in school but can have effects throughout life. For example, current research demonstrates the early and lasting effects of children's environments and experiences on brain development and cognition (Chugani, Phelps, & Mazziotta 1987; Caine & Caine 1991; Kuhl 1994). Studies show that "From infancy through about age 10, brain cells not only form most of the connections they will maintain throughout life but during this time they retain their greatest malleability" (Dana Alliance for Brain Initiatives 1996, 7).

Positive, supportive relationships, important during the earliest years of life, appear essential not only for cognitive development but also for healthy emotional development and social attachment (Bowlby 1969; Stern 1985). The preschool years are an optimum time for development of fundamental motor skills (Gallahue 1993), language development (Dyson & Genishi 1993), and other key foundational aspects of development that have life-long implications.

Recognition of the importance of the early years has heightened interest and support for early childhood education programs. A number of studies demonstrating long-term, positive consequences of participation in high-quality early childhood programs for children from low-income families influenced the expansion of

Head Start and public school prekindergarten (Lazar & Darlington 1982; Lee, Brooks-Gunn, & Schuur 1988; Schweinhart, Barnes, & Weikart 1993; Campbell & Ramey 1995). Several decades of research clearly demonstrate that high-quality, developmentally appropriate early childhood programs produce short- and long-term positive effects on children's cognitive and social development (Barnett 1995).

From a thorough review of the research on the long-term effects of early childhood education programs, Barnett concludes that "across all studies, the findings were relatively uniform and constitute overwhelming evidence that early childhood care and education can produce sizeable improvements in school success" (1995, 40). Children from low-income families who participated in high-quality preschool programs were significantly less likely to have been assigned to special education, retained in grade, engaged in crime, or to have dropped out of school. The longitudinal studies, in general, suggest positive consequences for programs that used an approach consistent with principles of developmentally appropriate practice (Lazar & Darlington 1982; Berreuta-Clement et al. 1984; Miller & Bizzell 1984; Schweinhart, Weikart, & Larner 1986; Schweinhart, Barnes, & Weikart 1993; Frede 1995; Schweinhart & Weikart 1996).

Research on the long-term effects of early childhood programs indicates that children who attend good-quality child care programs, even at very young ages, demonstrate positive outcomes, and children who attend poor-quality programs show negative effects (Vandell & Powers 1983; Phillips, McCartney, & Scarr 1987; Fields et al. 1988; Vandell, Henderson, & Wilson 1988; Arnett 1989; Vandell & Corasanti 1990; Burchinal et al. 1996). Specifically, children who experience high-quality, stable child care engage in more complex play, demonstrate more secure attachments to adults and other children, and score higher on measures of thinking ability and language development. High-quality child care can predict academic success, adjustment to school, and reduced behavioral problems for children in first grade (Howes 1988).

While the potential positive effects of high-quality child care are well documented, several large-scale evaluations of child care find that high-quality experiences are not the norm (Whitebook, Howes, & Phillips 1989; Howes, Phillips, & Whitebook 1992; Layzer, Goodson, & Moss 1993; Galinsky et al. 1994; Cost, Quality, & Child

Outcomes Study Team 1995). Each of these studies, which included observations of child care and preschool quality in several states, found that good-quality childcare that supports children's health and social and cognitive development is being provided in only about 15 percent of programs.

Of even greater concern was the large percentage of classrooms and family child care homes that were rated "barely adequate" or "inadequate" for quality. From 12 to 20 percent of the children were in settings that were considered dangerous to their health and safety and harmful to their social and cognitive development. An alarming number of infants and toddlers (35 to 40 percent) were found to be in unsafe settings (Cost, Quality, & Child Outcomes Study Team 1995).

Experiences during the earliest years of formal schooling are also formative. Studies demonstrate that children's success or failure during the first years of school often predicts the course of later schooling (Alexander & Entwisle 1988; Slavin, Karweit, & Madden 1989). A growing body of research indicates that more developmentally appropriate teaching in preschool and kindergarten predicts greater success in the early grades (Frede & Barnett 1992; Marcon 1992; Charlesworth et al. 1993).

As with preschool and child care, the observed quality of children's early schooling is uneven (Durkin 1987, 1990; Hiebert & Papierz 1990; Bryant, Clifford, & Peisner 1991; Carnegie Task Force 1996). For instance, in a statewide observational study of kindergarten classrooms, Durkin (1987) found that despite assessment results indicating considerable individual variation in children's literacy skills, which would call for various teaching strategies as well as individual and small-group work, teachers relied on one instructional strategy—whole-group, phonics instruction—and judged children who did not learn well with this one method as unready for first grade. Currently, too many children—especially children from low-income families and some minority groups—experience school failure, are retained in grade, get assigned to special education, and eventually drop out of school (Natriello, McDill, & Pallas 1990; Legters & Slavin 1992).

Results such as these indicate that while early childhood programs have the potential for producing positive and lasting effects on children, this potential will not be achieved unless more attention is paid to ensuring that all programs meet the highest standards of quality. As the number and type of early childhood programs increase, the need increases for a shared vision and agreed-upon standards of professional practice.

NAEYC's Commitment to Children

It is important to acknowledge at the outset the core values that undergird all of NAEYC's work. As stated in NAEYC's *Code of Ethical Conduct*, standards of professional practice in early childhood programs are based on commitment to certain fundamental values that are deeply rooted in the history of the early childhood field:

- appreciating childhood as a unique and valuable stage of the human life cycle (and valuing the quality of children's lives in the present, not just as preparation for the future)

- basing our work with children on knowledge of child development (and learning)

- appreciating and supporting the close ties between the child and the family

- recognizing that children are best understood in the context of family, culture, and society

- respecting the dignity, worth, and uniqueness of each individual (child, family member, and colleague)

- helping children and adults achieve their full potential in the context of relationships that are based on trust, respect, and positive regard (Feeney & Kipnis 1992, 3).

STATEMENT OF THE POSITION

Based on an enduring commitment to act on behalf of children, NAEYC's mission is to promote high-quality, developmentally appropriate programs for all children and their families. Because we define developmentally appropriate programs as programs that contribute to children's development, we must articulate our goals for children's development. The principles of practice advocated in this position statement are based on a set of goals for children: what we want for them, both in their present lives and as they develop to adulthood, and what personal characteristics should be fostered because these contribute to a peaceful, prosperous, and democratic society.

As we approach the 21st century, enormous changes are taking place in daily life and work. At the same time, certain human capacities will undoubtedly remain important elements in individual and societal well-being—no matter what economic or technological changes take place. With a recognition of both the continuities in human existence and the rapid changes in our world, broad agreement is emerging (e.g. Resnick 1996) that when today's children become adults they will need the ability to

- communicate well, respect others and engage with them to work through differences of opinion, and function well as members of a team

- analyze situations, make reasoned judgments, and solve new problems as they emerge

- access information through various modes, including spoken and written language, and intelligently employ complex tools and technologies as they are developed

- continue to learn new approaches, skills, and knowledge as conditions and needs change.

Clearly, people in the decades ahead will need, more than ever, fully developed literacy and numeracy skills, and these abilities are key goals of the educational process. In science, social studies (which includes history and geography), music and the visual arts, physical education and health, children need to acquire a body of knowledge and skills, as identified by those in the various disciplines (e.g. Bredekamp & Rosegrant 1995).

Besides acquiring a body of knowledge and skills, children must develop positive dispositions and attitudes. They need to understand that effort is necessary for achievement, for example, and they need to have curiosity and confidence in themselves as learners. Moreover, to live in a highly pluralistic society and world, young people need to develop a positive self-identity and a tolerance for others whose perspective and experience may be different from their own.

Beyond the shared goals of the early childhood field, every program for young children should establish its own goals in collaboration with families. All early childhood programs will not have identical goals; priorities may vary in some respects because programs serve a diversity of children and families. Such differences notwithstanding, NAEYC believes that all high quality, developmentally appropriate programs will have certain attributes in common. A high-quality early childhood program is one that provides a safe and nurturing environment that promotes the physical, social, emotional, aesthetic, intellectual, and language development of each child while being sensitive to the needs and preferences of families.

Many factors influence the quality of an early childhood program, including (but not limited to) the extent to which knowledge about how children develop and learn is applied in program practices. Developmentally appropriate programs are based on what is known about how children develop and learn; such programs promote the development and enhance the learning of each individual child served.

Developmentally appropriate practices result from the process of professionals making decisions about the well-being and education of children based on at least three important kinds of information or knowledge:

1. *what is known about child development and learning—* knowledge of age-related human characteristics that permits general predictions within an age range about what activities, materials, interactions, or experiences will be safe, healthy, interesting, achievable, and also challenging to children

2. *what is known about the strengths, interests, and needs of each individual child in the group* to be able to adapt for and be responsive to inevitable individual variation

3. *knowledge of the social and cultural contexts in which children live* to ensure that learning experiences are meaningful, relevant, and respectful for the participating children and their families.

Furthermore, each of these dimensions of knowledge—human development and learning, individual characteristics and experiences, and social and cultural contexts—is dynamic and changing, requiring that early childhood teachers remain learners throughout their careers.

An example illustrates the interrelatedness of these three dimensions of the decision-making process. Children all over the world acquire language at approximately the same period of the life span and in similar ways (Fernald 1992). But tremendous individual variation exists in the rate and pattern of language acquisition (Fenson et al. 1994). Also, children acquire the language or languages of the culture in which they live (Kuhl 1994). Thus, to adequately support a developmental task such as language acquisition, the teacher must draw on at least all three interrelated dimensions of knowledge to determine a developmentally appropriate strategy or intervention.

PRINCIPLES OF CHILD DEVELOPMENT AND LEARNING THAT INFORM DEVELOPMENTALLY APPROPRIATE PRACTICE

Taken together, these core values define NAEYC's basic commitment to children and underlie its position on developmentally appropriate practice.

Developmentally appropriate practice is based on knowledge about how children develop and learn. As Katz states, "In a developmental approach to curriculum design, . . . [decisions] about what should be learned and how it would best be learned depend on what we know of the learner's developmental status and our understanding of the relationships between early experience and subsequent development" (1995, 109). To guide their decisions about practice, all early childhood teachers need to understand the developmental changes that typically occur in the years from birth through age eight and beyond, variations in development that may occur, and how best to support children's learning and development during these years.

A complete discussion of the knowledge base that informs early childhood practice is beyond the scope of this document (see, for example, Seefeldt 1992; Sroufe, Cooper, & DeHart 1992; Kostelnik, Soderman, & Whiren 1993; Spodek 1993; Berk 1996). Because development and learning are so complex, no one theory is sufficient to explain these phenomena. However, a broad-based review of the literature on early childhood education generates a set of principles to inform early childhood practice. *Principles* are generalizations that are sufficiently reliable that they should be taken into account when making decisions (Katz & Chard 1989; Katz 1995). Following is a list of empirically based principles of child development and learning that inform and guide decisions about developmentally appropriate practice.

1. **Domains of children's development—physical, social, emotional, and cognitive—are closely related. Development in one domain influences and is influenced by development in other domains.** Development in one domain can limit or facilitate development in others (Sroufe, Cooper, & DeHart 1992; Kostelnik, Soderman, & Whiren 1993). For example, when babies begin to crawl or walk, their ability to explore the world expands, and their mobility, in turn, affects their cognitive development. Likewise, children's language skill affects their ability to establish social relationships with adults and other children, just as their skill in social interaction can support or impede their language development. Because developmental domains are interrelated, educators should be aware of and use these interrelationships to organize children's learning experiences in ways that help children develop optimally in all areas and that make meaningful connections across domains. Recognition of the connections across developmental domains is also useful for curriculum planning with the various age groups represented in the early childhood period. Curriculum with infants and toddlers is almost solely driven by the need to support their healthy development in all domains. During the primary grades, curriculum planning attempts to help children develop conceptual understandings that apply across related subject-matter disciplines.

2. **Development occurs in a relatively orderly sequence, with later abilities, skills, and knowledge building on those already acquired.** Human development research indicates that relatively stable, predictable sequences of growth and change occur in children during the first nine years of life (Piaget 1952; Erikson 1963; Dyson & Genishi 1993; Gallahue 1993; Case & Okamoto 1996). Predictable changes occur in all domains of development—physical, emotional, social, language, and cognitive—although the ways that these changes are manifest and the meaning attached to them may vary in different cultural contexts. Knowledge of typical development of children within the age span served by the program provides a general framework to guide how teachers prepare the learning environment and plan realistic curriculum goals and objectives and appropriate experiences.

3. **Development proceeds at varying rates from child to child as well as unevenly within different areas of each child's functioning.** Individual variation has at least two

dimensions: the inevitable variability around the average or normative course of development and the uniqueness of each person as an individual (Sroufe, Cooper, & DeHart 1992). Each child is a unique person with an individual pattern and timing of growth, as well as individual personality, temperament, learning style, and experiential and family background. All children have their own strengths, needs, and interests; for some children, special learning and developmental needs or abilities are identified. Given the enormous variation among children of the same chronological age, a child's age must be recognized as only a crude index of developmental maturity.

Recognition that individual variation is not only to be expected but also valued requires that decisions about curriculum and adults' interactions with children be as individualized as possible. Emphasis on individual appropriateness is not the same as "individualism." Rather, this recognition requires that children be considered not solely as members of an age group, expected to perform to a predetermined norm and without adaptation to individual variation of any kind. Having high expectations for all children is important, but rigid expectations of group norms do not reflect what is known about real differences in individual development and learning during the early years. Group-norm expectancy can be especially harmful for children with special learning and developmental needs (NEGP 1991; Mallory 1992; Wolery, Strain, & Bailey 1992).

4. **Early experiences have both cumulative and delayed effects on individual children's development; optimal periods exist for certain types of development and learning.** Children's early experiences, either positive or negative, are cumulative in the sense that if an experience occurs occasionally, it may have minimal effects. If positive or negative experiences occur frequently, however, they can have powerful, lasting, even "snowballing," effects (Katz & Chard 1989; Kostelnik, Soderman, & Whiren 1993; Wieder & Greenspan 1993). For example, a child's social experiences with other children in the preschool years help him develop social skills and confidence that enable him to make friends in the early school years, and these experiences further enhance the child's social competence. Conversely, children who fail to develop minimal social competence and are neglected or rejected by peers are at significant risk to drop out of school, become delinquent, and experience

mental health problems in adulthood (Asher, Hymel, & Renshaw 1984; Parker & Asher 1987).

Similar patterns can be observed in babies whose cries and other attempts at communication are regularly responded to, thus enhancing their own sense of efficacy and increasing communicative competence. Likewise, when children have or do not have early literacy experiences, such as being read to regularly, their later success in learning to read is affected accordingly. Perhaps most convincing is the growing body of research demonstrating that social and sensorimotor experiences during the first three years directly affect neurological development of the brain, with important and lasting implications for children's capacity to learn (Dana Alliance for Brain Initiatives 1996).

Early experiences can also have delayed effects, either positive or negative, on subsequent development. For instance, some evidence suggests that reliance on extrinsic rewards (such as candy or money) to shape children's behavior, a strategy that can be very effective in the short term, under certain circumstances lessens children's intrinsic motivation to engage in the rewarded behavior in the long term (Dweck 1986; Kohn 1993). For example, paying children to read books may over time undermine their desire to read for their own enjoyment and edification.

At certain points in the life span, some kinds of learning and development occur most efficiently. For example, the first three years of life appear to be an optimal period for verbal language development (Kuhl 1994). Although delays in language development due to physical or environmental deficits can be ameliorated later on, such intervention usually requires considerable effort. Similarly, the preschool years appear to be optimum for fundamental motor development (i.e. fundamental motor skills are more easily and efficiently acquired at this age) (Gallahue 1995). Children who have many opportunities and adult support to practice simple motor skills (running, jumping, hopping, skipping) during this period have the cumulative benefit of being better able to acquire more sophisticated, complex motor skills (balancing on a beam or riding a two-wheel bike) in subsequent years. On the other hand, children whose early motor experiences are severely limited may struggle to acquire physical competence and may also experience delayed effects when attempting to participate in sports or personal fitness activities later in life.

5. **Development proceeds in predictable directions toward greater complexity, organization, and internalization.** Learning during early childhood proceeds from behavioral knowledge to symbolic or representational knowledge (Bruner 1983). For example, children learn to navigate their homes and other familiar settings long before they can understand the words *left* and *right* or read a map of the house. Developmentally appropriate programs provide opportunities for children to broaden and deepen their behavioral knowledge by providing a variety of firsthand experiences and by helping children acquire symbolic knowledge through representing their experiences in a variety of media, such as drawing, painting, construction of models, dramatic play, verbal and written descriptions (Katz 1995).

   Even very young children are able to use various media to represent their understanding of concepts. Furthermore, through representation of their knowledge, the knowledge itself is enhanced (Edwards, Gandini, & Forman 1993; Malaguzzi 1993; Forman 1994). Representational modes and media also vary with the age of the child. For instance, most learning for infants and toddlers is sensory and motoric, but by age two children use one object to stand for another in play (a block for a phone or a spoon for a guitar).

6. **Development and learning occur in and are influenced by multiple social and cultural contexts.** Bronfenbrenner (1979, 1989, 1993) provides an ecological model for understanding human development. He explains that children's development is best understood within the sociocultural context of the family, educational setting, community, and broader society. These various contexts are interrelated, and all have an impact on the developing child. For example, even a child in a loving, supportive family within a strong, healthy community is affected by the biases of the larger society, such as racism or sexism, and may show the effects of negative stereotyping and discrimination.

   We define *culture* as the customary beliefs and patterns of and for behavior, both explicit and implicit, that are passed on to future generations by the society they live in and/or by a social, religious, or ethnic group within it. Because culture is often discussed in the context of diversity or multiculturalism, people fail to recognize the powerful role that culture plays in influencing the development of *all* children. Every culture

structures and interprets children's behavior and development
(Edwards & Gandini 1989; Tobin, Wu, & Davidson 1989;
Rogoff et al. 1993). As Bowman states, "Rules of development
are the same for all children, but social contexts shape children's development into different configurations" (1994, 220).
Early childhood teachers need to understand the influence of
sociocultural contexts on learning, recognize children's developing competence, and accept a variety of ways for children to
express their developmental achievements (Vygotsky 1978;
Wertsch 1985; Forman, Minick, & Stone 1993; New 1993,
1994; Bowman & Stott 1994; Mallory & New 1994a; Phillips
1994; Bruner 1996; Wardle 1996).

Teachers should learn about the culture of the majority of
the children they serve if that culture differs from their own.
However, recognizing that development and learning are influenced by social and cultural contexts does not require teachers to
understand all the nuances of every cultural group they may
encounter in their practice; this would be an impossible task.
Rather, this fundamental recognition sensitizes teachers to the
need to acknowledge how their own cultural experience shapes
their perspective and to realize that multiple perspectives, in
addition to their own, must be considered in decisions about
children's development and learning.

Children are capable of learning to function in more than
one cultural context simultaneously. However, if teachers set
low expectations for children based on their home culture and
language, children cannot develop and learn optimally.
Education should be an additive process. For example,
children whose primary language is not English should be able
to learn English without being forced to give up their home
language (NAEYC 1996a). Likewise, children who speak
only English benefit from learning another language. The goal
is that all children learn to function well in the society as
a whole and move comfortably among groups of people who
come from both similar and dissimilar backgrounds.

7. **Children are active learners, drawing on direct physical
   and social experience as well as culturally transmitted
   knowledge to construct their own understandings of the
   world around them.**   Children contribute to their own development and learning as they strive to make meaning out of their
   daily experiences in the home, the early childhood program,
   and the community. Principles of developmentally appropriate

practice are based on several prominent theories that view intellectual development from a constructivist, interactive perspective (Dewey 1916; Piaget 1952; Vygotsky 1978; DeVries & Kohlberg 1990; Rogoff 1990; Gardner 1991; Kamii & Ewing 1996).

From birth, children are actively engaged in constructing their own understandings from their experiences, and these understandings are mediated by and clearly linked to the sociocultural context. Young children actively learn from observing and participating with other children and adults, including parents and teachers. Children need to form their own hypotheses and keep trying them out through social interaction, physical manipulation, and their own thought processes—observing what happens, reflecting on their findings, asking questions, and formulating answers. When objects, events, and other people challenge the working model that the child has mentally constructed, the child is forced to adjust the model or alter the mental structures to account for the new information. Throughout early childhood, the child in processing new experiences continually reshapes, expands, and reorganizes mental structures (Piaget 1952; Vygotsky 1978; Case & Okamoto 1996). When teachers and other adults use various strategies to encourage children to reflect on their experiences by planning beforehand and "revisiting" afterward, the knowledge and understanding gained from the experience is deepened (Copple, Sigel, & Saunders 1984; Edwards, Gandini, & Forman 1993; Stremmel & Fu 1993; Hohmann & Weikart 1995).

In the statement of this principle, the term "physical and social experience" is used in the broadest sense to include children's exposure to physical knowledge, learned through first-hand experience of using objects (observing that a ball thrown in the air falls down), and social knowledge, including the vast body of culturally acquired and transmitted knowledge that children need to function in the world. For example, children progressively construct their own understanding of various symbols, but the symbols they use (such as the alphabet or numerical system) are the ones used within their culture and transmitted to them by adults.

In recent years, discussions of cognitive development have at times become polarized (see Seifert 1993). Piaget's theory stressed that development of certain cognitive structures was a necessary prerequisite to learning (i.e. development precedes learning), while other research has demonstrated that instruction in specific concepts or strategies can facilitate development of more mature cognitive structures (learning precedes development) (Vygotsky 1978; Gelman & Baillargeon 1983). Current attempts to resolve this apparent dichotomy (Seifert 1993; Sameroff & McDonough 1994; Case & Okamoto 1996) acknowledge that essentially both theoretical perspectives are correct in explaining aspects of cognitive development during early childhood. Strategic teaching, of course, can enhance children's learning. Yet, direct instruction may be totally ineffective; it fails when it is not attuned to the cognitive capacities and knowledge of the child at that point in development.

8. **Development and learning result from interaction of biological maturation and the environment, which includes both the physical and social worlds that children live in.** The simplest way to express this principle is that human beings are products of both heredity and environment and these forces are interrelated. Behaviorists focus on the environmental influences that determine learning, while maturationists emphasize the unfolding of predetermined, hereditary characteristics. Each perspective is true to some extent, and yet neither perspective is sufficient to explain learning or development. More often today, development is viewed as the result of an interactive, transactional process between the growing, changing individual and their experiences in the social and physical worlds (Scarr & McCartney 1983; Plomin 1994a,b). For example, a child's genetic makeup may predict healthy growth, but inadequate nutrition in the early years of life may keep this potential from being fulfilled. Or a severe disability, whether inherited or environmentally caused, may be ameliorated through systematic, appropriate intervention. Likewise, a child's inherited temperament—whether a predisposition to be wary or outgoing—shapes and is shaped by how other children and adults communicate with that child.

9. **Play is an important vehicle for children's social, emotional, and cognitive development, as well as a reflection of their development.** Understanding that children are active constructors of knowledge and that development and learning are the result of interactive processes, early childhood teachers recognize that children's play is a highly supportive context for these developing processes (Piaget 1952; Fein 1981; Bergen 1988; Smilansky & Shefatya 1990; Fromberg 1992; Berk &

Winsler 1995). Play gives children opportunities to understand the world, interact with others in social ways, express and control emotions, and develop their symbolic capabilities. Children's play gives adults insights into children's development and opportunities to support the development of new strategies. Vygotsky (1978) believed that play leads development, with written language growing out of oral language through the vehicle of symbolic play that promotes the development of symbolic representation abilities. Play provides a context for children to practice newly acquired skills and also to function on the edge of their developing capacities to take on new social roles, attempt novel or challenging tasks, and solve complex problems that they would not (or could not) otherwise do (Mallory & New 1994b).

Research demonstrates the importance of sociodramatic play as a tool for learning curriculum content with three- through six-year-old children. When teachers provide a thematic organization for play; offer appropriate props, space, and time; and become involved in the play by extending and elaborating on children's ideas, children's language and literacy skills can be enhanced (Levy, Schaefer, & Phelps 1986; Schrader 1989, 1990; Morrow 1990; Pramling 1991; Levy, Wolfgang, & Koorland 1992).

In addition to supporting cognitive development, play serves important functions in children's physical, emotional, and social development (Herron & Sutton-Smith 1971). Children express and represent their ideas, thoughts, and feelings when engaged in symbolic play. During play a child can learn to deal with emotions, to interact with others, to resolve conflicts, and to gain a sense of competence—all in the safety that only play affords. Through play, children also can develop their imaginations and creativity. Therefore, child-initiated, teacher-supported play is an essential component of developmentally appropriate practice (Fein & Rivkin 1986).

10. **Development advances when children have opportunities to practice newly acquired skills as well as when they experience a challenge just beyond the level of their present mastery.** Research demonstrates that children need to be able to successfully negotiate learning tasks most of the time if they are to maintain motivation and persistence (Lary 1990; Brophy 1992). Confronted by repeated failure, most

children will simply stop trying. So most of the time, teachers should give young children tasks that they can accomplish with effort and present them with content that is accessible at their level of understanding. At the same time, children continually gravitate to situations and stimuli that give them the chance to work at their "growing edge" (Berk & Winsler 1995; Bodrova & Leong 1996). Moreover, in a task just beyond the child's independent reach, the adult and more-competent peers contribute significantly to development by providing the supportive "scaffolding" that allows the child to take the next step.

Development and learning are dynamic processes requiring that adults understand the continuum, observe children closely to match curriculum and teaching to children's emerging competencies, needs, and interests, and then help children move forward by targeting educational experiences to the edge of children's changing capacities so as to challenge but not frustrate them. Human beings, especially children, are highly motivated to understand what they almost, but not quite, comprehend and to master what they can almost, but not quite, do (White 1965; Vygotsky 1978). The principle of learning is that children can do things first in a supportive context and then later independently and in a variety of contexts. Rogoff (1990) describes the process of adult-assisted learning as "guided participation" to emphasize that children actively collaborate with others to move to more complex levels of understanding and skill.

11. **Children demonstrate different modes of knowing and learning and different ways of representing what they know.** For some time, learning theorists and developmental psychologists have recognized that human beings come to understand the world in many ways and that individuals tend to have preferred or stronger modes of learning. Studies of differences in learning modalities have contrasted visual, auditory, or tactile learners. Other work has identified learners as field-dependent or independent (Witkin 1962). Gardner (1983) expanded on this concept by theorizing that human beings possess at least seven "intelligences." In addition to having the ones traditionally emphasized in schools, linguistic and logical-mathematical, individuals are more or less proficient in at least these other areas: musical, spatial, bodily kinesthetic, intrapersonal, and interpersonal.

Malaguzzi (1993) used the metaphor of "100 languages" to describe the diverse modalities through which children come to understand the world and represent their knowledge. The processes of representing their understanding can, with the assistance of teachers, help children deepen, improve, and expand their understanding (Copple, Sigel, & Saunders 1984; Forman 1994; Katz 1995). The principle of diverse modalities implies that teachers should provide not only opportunities for individual children to use their preferred modes of learning to capitalize on their strengths (Hale-Benson 1986) but also opportunities to help children develop in the modes or intelligences in which they may not be as strong.

12. **Children develop and learn best in the context of a community where they are safe and valued, their physical needs are met, and they feel psychologically secure.** Maslow (1954) conceptualized a hierarchy of needs in which learning was not considered possible unless physical and psychological needs for safety and security were first met. Because children's physical health and safety too often are threatened today, programs for young children must not only provide adequate health, safety, and nutrition but may also need to ensure more comprehensive services, such as physical, dental, and mental health and social services (NASBE 1991; US Department of Health & Human Services 1996). In addition, children's development in all areas is influenced by their ability to establish and maintain a limited number of positive, consistent primary relationships with adults and other children (Bowlby 1969; Stern 1985; Garbarino et al. 1992). These primary relationships begin in the family but extend over time to include children's teachers and members of the community; therefore, practices that are developmentally appropriate address children's physical, social, and emotional needs as well as their intellectual development.

GUIDELINES FOR DECISIONS ABOUT DEVELOPMENTALLY APPROPRIATE PRACTICE

A linear listing of principles of child development and learning, such as the above, cannot do justice to the complexity of the phenomena that it attempts to describe and explain. Just as all domains of development and learning are interrelated, so, too, there are relationships among the principles. Similarly, the following guidelines for practice do not match up one-to-one with the principles. Instead, early childhood professionals draw on all these fundamental ideas (as well as many others) when making decisions about their practice.

An understanding of the nature of development and learning during the early childhood years, from birth through age eight, generates guidelines that inform the practices of early childhood educators. Developmentally appropriate practice requires that teachers integrate the many dimensions of their knowledge base. They must know about child development and the implications of this knowledge for how to teach the content of the curriculum— what to teach and when—how to assess what children have learned, and how to adapt curriculum and instruction to children's individual strengths, needs, and interests. Further, they must know the particular children they teach and their families and be knowledgeable as well about the social and cultural context.

The following guidelines address five interrelated dimensions of early childhood professional practice: creating a caring community of learners, teaching to enhance development and learning, constructing appropriate curriculum, assessing children's development and learning, and establishing reciprocal relationships with families. (The word *teacher* is used to refer to any adult responsible for a group of children in any early childhood program, including infant/toddler caregivers, family child care providers, and specialists in other disciplines who fulfill the role of teacher.)

Examples of appropriate and inappropriate practice in relation to each of these dimensions are given for infants and toddlers (Part 3, pp. 72–90), children three through five (Part 4, pp. 123–35), and children six through eight (Part 5, pp. 161–78). In the references at the end of each part, readers will be able to find fuller discussion of the points summarized here and strategies for implementation.

1. **Creating a caring community of learners.**   Developmentally appropriate practices occur within a context that supports the development of relationships between adults and children, among children, among teachers, and between teachers and families. Such a community reflects what is known about the social construction of knowledge and the importance of establishing a caring, inclusive community in which all children can develop and learn.

A. The early childhood setting functions as a community of learners in which all participants consider and contribute to each other's well-being and learning.

B. Consistent, positive relationships with a limited number of adults and other children are a fundamental determinant of healthy human development and provide the context for children to learn about themselves and their world and also how to develop positive, constructive relationships with other people. The early childhood classroom is a community in which each child is valued. Children learn to respect and acknowledge differences in abilities and talents and to value each person for their strengths.

C. Social relationships are an important context for learning. Each child has strengths or interests that contribute to the overall functioning of the group. When children have opportunities to play together, work on projects in small groups, and talk with other children and adults, their own development and learning are enhanced. Interacting with other children in small groups provides a context for children to operate on the edge of their developing capacities. The learning environment enables children to construct understanding through interactions with adults and other children.

D. The learning environment is designed to protect children's health and safety and is supportive of children's physiological needs for activity, sensory stimulation, fresh air, rest, and nourishment. The program provides a balance of rest and active movement for children throughout the program day. Outdoor experiences are provided for children of all ages. The program protects children's psychological safety; that is, children feel secure, relaxed, and comfortable rather than disengaged, frightened, worried, or stressed.

E. Children experience an organized environment and an orderly routine that provides an overall structure in which learning takes place; the environment is dynamic and changing but predictable and comprehensible from a child's point of view. The learning environment provides a variety of materials and opportunities for children to have firsthand, meaningful experiences.

2. **Teaching to enhance development and learning.** Adults are responsible for ensuring children's healthy development

and learning. From birth, relationships with adults are critical determinants of children's healthy social and emotional development and serve as mediators of language and intellectual development. At the same time, children are active constructors of their own understanding, who benefit from initiating and regulating their own learning activities and interacting with peers. Therefore, early childhood teachers strive to achieve an optimal balance between children's self-initiated learning and adult guidance or support.

Teachers accept responsibility for actively supporting children's development and provide occasions for children to acquire important knowledge and skills. Teachers use their knowledge of child development and learning to identify the range of activities, materials, and learning experiences that are appropriate for a group or individual child. This knowledge is used in conjunction with knowledge of the context and understanding about individual children's growth patterns, strengths, needs, interests, and experiences to design the curriculum and learning environment and guide teachers' interactions with children. The following guidelines describe aspects of the teachers' role in making decisions about practice:

A. Teachers respect, value, and accept children and treat them with dignity at all times.

B. Teachers make it a priority to know each child well.
    (1) Teachers establish positive, personal relationships with children to foster the child's development and keep themselves informed about the child's needs and potentials. Teachers listen to children and adapt their responses to children's differing needs, interests, styles, and abilities.
    (2) Teachers continually observe children's spontaneous play and interaction with the physical environment and with other children to learn about their interests, abilities, and developmental progress. On the basis of this information, teachers plan experiences that enhance children's learning and development.
    (3) Understanding that children develop and learn in the context of their families and communities, teachers establish relationships with families that increase their knowledge of children's lives outside the classroom and their awareness of the perspectives and priorities of those individuals most significant in the child's life.

(4) Teachers are alert to signs of undue stress and traumatic events in children's lives and aware of effective strategies to reduce stress and support the development of resilience.

(5) Teachers are responsible at all times for all children under their supervision and plan for children's increasing development of self-regulation abilities.

C. Teachers create an intellectually engaging, responsive environment to promote each child's learning and development.

(1) Teachers use their knowledge about children in general and children in the group in particular as well as their familiarity with what children need to learn and develop in each curriculum area to organize the environment and plan curriculum and teaching strategies.

(2) Teachers provide children with a rich variety of experiences, projects, materials, problems, and ideas to explore and investigate, ensuring that these are worthy of children's attention.

(3) Teachers provide children with opportunities to make meaningful choices and time to explore through active involvement. Teachers offer children the choice to participate in a small-group or a solitary activity, assist and guide children who are not yet able to use and enjoy child-choice activity periods, and provide opportunities for practice of skills as a self-chosen activity.

(4) Teachers organize the daily and weekly schedule and allocate time so as to provide children with extended blocks of time in which to engage in play, projects, and/or study in integrated curriculum.

D. Teachers make plans to enable children to attain key curriculum goals across various disciplines, such as language arts, mathematics, social studies, science, art, music, physical education, and health (see "Constructing appropriate curriculum," pp. 20–21).

(1) Teachers incorporate a wide variety of experiences, materials and equipment, and teaching strategies in constructing curriculum to accommodate a broad range of children's individual differences in prior experiences, maturation rates, styles of learning, needs, and interests.

    (2) Teachers bring each child's home culture and language into the shared culture of the school so that the unique contributions of each group are recognized and valued by others.

    (3) Teachers are prepared to meet identified special needs of individual children, including children with disabilities and those who exhibit unusual interests and skills. Teachers use all the strategies identified here, consult with appropriate specialists, and see that the child gets the specialized services require.

E. Teachers foster children's collaboration with peers on interesting, important enterprises.

    (1) Teachers promote children's productive collaboration without taking over to the extent that children lose interest.

    (2) Teachers use a variety of ways of flexibly grouping children for the purposes of instruction, supporting collaboration among children and building a sense of community. At various times, children have opportunities to work individually, in small groups, and with the whole group.

F. Teachers develop, refine, and use a wide repertoire of teaching strategies to enhance children's learning and development.

    (1) To help children develop their initiative, teachers encourage them to choose and plan their own learning activities.

    (2) Teachers pose problems, ask questions, and make comments and suggestions that stimulate children's thinking and extend their learning.

    (3) Teachers extend the range of children's interests and the scope of their thought through presenting novel experiences and introducing stimulating ideas, problems, experiences, or hypotheses.

    (4) To sustain an individual child's effort or engagement in purposeful activities, teachers select from a range of strategies, including but not limited to modeling, demonstrating specific skills, and providing information, focused attention, physical proximity, verbal encouragement, reinforcement and other behavioral procedures, as well as additional structure and modification of equipment or schedules as needed.

(5) Teachers coach and/or directly guide children in the acquisition of specific skills as needed.

(6) Teachers calibrate the complexity and challenge of activities to suit children's level of skill and knowedge, increasing the challenge as children gain competence and understanding.

(7) Teachers provide cues and other forms of "scaffolding" that enable the child to succeed in a task that is just beyond their ability to complete alone.

(8) To strengthen children's sense of competence and confidence as learners, motivation to persist, and willingness to take risks, teachers provide experiences for children to be genuinely successful and to be challenged.

(9) To enhance children's conceptual understanding, teachers use various strategies that encourage children to reflect on and "revisit" their learning experiences.

G. Teachers facilitate the development of responsibility and self-regulation in children.

(1) Teachers set clear, consistent, and fair limits for children's behavior and hold children accountable to standards of acceptable behavior. To the extent that children are able, teachers engage them in developing rules and procedures for behavior of class members.

(2) Teachers redirect children to more acceptable behavior or activity or use children's mistakes as learning opportunities, patiently reminding children of rules and their rationale as needed.

(3) Teachers listen and acknowledge children's feelings and frustrations, respond with respect, guide children to resolve conflicts, and model skills that help children to solve their own problems.

3. **Constructing appropriate curriculum.**   The content of the early childhood curriculum is determined by many factors, including the subject matter of the disciplines, social or cultural values, and parental input. In developmentally appropriate programs, decisions about curriculum content also take into consideration the age and experience of the learners. Achieving success for all children depends, among other essentials, on providing a challenging, interesting, developmentally appropriate curriculum. NAEYC does not

endorse specific curricula. However, one purpose of these guidelines is as a framework for making decisions about developing curriculum or selecting a curriculum model. Teachers who use a validated curriculum model benefit from the evidence of its effectiveness and the accumulated wisdom and experience of others.

In some respects, the curriculum strategies of many teachers today do not demand enough of children and in other ways demand too much of the wrong thing. On the one hand, narrowing the curriculum to those basic skills that can be easily measured on multiple-choice tests diminishes the intellectual challenge for many children. Such intellectually impoverished curriculum underestimates the true competence of children, which has been demonstrated to be much higher than is often assumed (Gelman & Baillargeon 1983; Gelman & Meck 1983; Edwards, Gandini, & Forman 1993; Resnick 1996). Watered-down, oversimplified curriculum leaves many children unchallenged, bored, uninterested, or unmotivated. In such situations, children's experiences are marked by a great many missed opportunities for learning.

On the other hand, curriculum expectations in the early years of schooling sometimes are not appropriate for the age groups served. When next-grade expectations of mastery of basic skills are routinely pushed down to the previous grade and whole group and teacher-led instruction is the dominant teaching strategy, children who cannot sit still and attend to teacher lectures or who are bored and unchallenged or frustrated by doing workbook pages for long periods of time are mislabeled as immature, disruptive, or unready for school (Shepard & Smith 1988). Constructing appropriate curriculum requires attention to at least the following guidelines for practice:

A. Developmentally appropriate curriculum provides for all areas of a child's development: physical, emotional, social, linguistic, aesthetic, and cognitive.

B. Curriculum includes a broad range of content across disciplines that is socially relevant, intellectually engaging, and personally meaningful to children.

C. Curriculum builds upon what children already know and are able to do (activating prior knowledge) to consolidate their learning and to foster their acquisition of new concepts and skills.

D. Effective curriculum plans frequently integrate across traditional subject-matter divisions to help children make meaningful connections and provide opportunities for rich conceptual development; focusing on one subject is also a valid strategy at times.

E. Curriculum promotes the development of knowledge and understanding, processes and skills, as well as the dispositions to use and apply skills and to go on learning.

F. Curriculum content has intellectual integrity, reflecting the key concepts and tools of inquiry of recognized disciplines in ways that are accessible and achievable for young children, ages three through eight (e.g. Bredekamp & Rosegrant 1992, 1995). Children directly participate in study of the disciplines, for instance, by conducting scientific experiments, writing, performing, solving mathematical problems, collecting and analyzing data, collecting oral history, and performing other roles of experts in the disciplines.

G. Curriculum provides opportunities to support children's home culture and language while also developing all children's abilities to participate in the shared culture of the program and the community.

H. Curriculum goals are realistic and attainable for most children in the designated age range for which they are designed.

I. When used, technology is physically and philosophically integrated in the classroom curriculum and teaching. (See "NAEYC Position Statement: Technology and Young Children—Ages Three through Eight" [NAEYC 1996b].)

4. **Assessing children's learning and development.** Assessment of individual children's development and learning is essential for planning and implementing appropriate curriculum. In developmentally appropriate programs, assessment and curriculum are integrated, with teachers continually engaging in observational assessment for the purpose of improving teaching and learning.

Accurate assessment of young children is difficult because their development and learning are rapid, uneven, episodic, and embedded within specific cultural and linguistic contexts. Too often, inaccurate and inappropriate assessment measures have been used to label, track, or otherwise harm young children. Developmentally appropriate assessment practices are based on the following guidelines:

A. Assessment of young children's progress and achievements is ongoing, strategic, and purposeful. The results of assessment are used to benefit children—in adapting curriculum and teaching to meet the developmental and learning needs of children, communicating with the child's family, and evaluating the program's effectiveness for the purpose of improving the program.

B. The content of assessments reflects progress toward important learning and developmental goals. The program has a systematic plan for collecting and using assessment information that is integrated with curriculum planning.

C. The methods of assessment are appropriate to the age and experiences of young children. Therefore, assessment of young children relies heavily on the results of observations of children's development, descriptive data, collections of representative work by children, and demonstrated performance during authentic, not contrived, activities. Input from families as well as children's evaluations of their own work are part of the overall assessment strategy.

D. Assessments are tailored to a specific purpose and used only for the purpose for which they have been demonstrated to produce reliable, valid information.

E. Decisions that have a major impact on children, such as enrollment or placement, are never made on the basis of a single developmental assessment or screening device but are based on multiple sources of relevant information, particularly observations by teachers and parents.

F. To identify children who have special learning or developmental needs and to plan appropriate curriculum and teaching for them, developmental assessments and observations are used.

G. Assessment recognizes individual variation in learners and allows for differences in styles and rates of learning. Assessment takes into consideration such factors as the child's facility in English, stage of language acquisition, and whether the child has had the time and opportunity to develop proficiency in their home language as well as in English.

H. Assessment legitimately addresses not only what children can do independently but what they can do with assistance from other children or adults. Teachers study children as individuals as well as in relationship to groups by documenting group projects and other collaborative work. (For a more complete discussion of principles of appropriate assessment, see the position statement *Guidelines for Appropriate Curriculum Content and Assessment for Children Ages 3 through 8* [NAEYC & NAECS/SDE 1992]; see also Shepard 1994.)

5. **Establishing reciprocal relationships with families.** Developmentally appropriate practices derive from deep knowledge of individual children and the context within which they develop and learn. The younger the child, the more necessary it is for professionals to acquire this knowledge through relationships with children's families. The traditional approach to families has been a parent education orientation in which the professionals see themselves as knowing what is best for children and view parents as needing to be educated. There is also the limited view of parent involvement that sees PTA membership as the primary goal. These approaches do not adequately convey the complexity of the partnership between teachers and parents that is a fundamental element of good practice (Powell 1994).

When the parent education approach is criticized in favor of a more family-centered approach, this shift may be misunderstood to mean that parents dictate all program content and professionals abdicate responsibility, doing whatever parents want regardless of whether professionals agree that it is in their children's best interests. Either of these extremes oversimplifies the importance of relationships with families and fails to provide the kind of environment in which parents and professionals work together to achieve shared goals for children; such programs with this focus are characterized by at least the following guidelines for practice:

A. Reciprocal relationships between teachers and families require mutual respect, cooperation, shared responsibility, and negotiation of conflicts toward achievement of shared goals.

B. Early childhood teachers work in collaborative partnerships with families, establishing and maintaining regular, frequent two-way communication with children's parents.

C. Parents are welcome in the program and participate in decisions about their children's care and education. Parents observe and participate and serve in decision-making roles in the program.

D. Teachers acknowledge parents' choices and goals for children and respond with sensitivity and respect to parents' preferences and concerns without abdicating professional responsibility to children.

E. Teachers and parents share their knowledge of the child and understanding of children's development and learning as part of day-to-day communication and planned conferences. Teachers support families in ways that maximally promote family decision-making capabilities and competence.

F. To ensure more accurate and complete information, the program involves families in assessing and planning for individual children.

G. The program links families with a range of services, based on identified resources, priorities, and concerns.

H. Teachers, parents, programs, social service and health agencies, and consultants who may have educational responsibility for the child at different times should, with family participation, share developmental information about children as they pass from one level or program to another.

MOVING FROM EITHER/OR TO BOTH/AND THINKING IN EARLY CHILDHOOD PRACTICE

Some critical reactions to NAEYC's (1987) position statement on developmentally appropriate practice reflect a recurring tendency in the American discourse on education: the polarizing into *either/or* choices of many questions that are more fruitfully seen as *both/ands*. For example, heated debates have broken out about whether children in the early grades should receive whole language or phonics instruction, when, in fact, the two approaches are quite compatible and most effective in combination.

It is true that there are practices that are clearly inappropriate for early childhood professionals—use of physical punishment or disparaging verbal comments about children, discriminating against children or their families, and many other examples that could be cited (see Parts 3, 4, and 5 for examples relevant to different age groups). However, most questions about practice require more complex responses. It is not that children need food or water; they need both.

To illustrate the many ways that early childhood practice draws on *both/and* thinking and to convey some of the complexity and interrelationship among the principles that guide our practice, we offer the following statements as examples:

- Children construct their own understanding of concepts, and they benefit from instruction by more competent peers and adults.

- Children benefit from opportunities to see connections across disciplines through integration of curriculum and from opportunities to engage in in-depth study within a content area.

- Children benefit from predictable structure and orderly routine in the learning environment and from the teacher's flexibility and spontaneity in responding to their emerging ideas, needs, and interests.

- Children benefit from opportunities to make meaningful choices about what they will do and learn and from having a clear understanding of the boundaries within which choices are permissible.

- Children benefit from situations that challenge them to work at the edge of their developing capacities and from ample opportunities to practice newly acquired skills and to acquire the disposition to persist.

- Children benefit from opportunities to collaborate with their peers and acquire a sense of being part of a community and from being treated as individuals with their own strengths, interests, and needs.

- Children need to develop a positive sense of their own self-identity and respect for other people whose perspectives and experiences may be different from their own.

- Children have enormous capacities to learn and almost boundless curiosity about the world, and they have recognized, age-related limits on their cognitive and linguistic capacities.

- Children benefit from engaging in self-initiated, spontaneous play and from teacher-planned and -structured activities, projects, and experiences.

The above list is not exhaustive. Many more examples could be cited to convey the interrelationships among the principles of child development and learning or among the guidelines for early childhood practice.

POLICIES ESSENTIAL FOR ACHIEVING DEVELOPMENTALLY APPROPRIATE EARLY CHILDHOOD PROGRAMS

Early childhood professionals working in diverse situations with varying levels of funding and resources are responsible for implementing practices that are developmentally appropriate for the children they serve. Regardless of the resources available, professionals have an ethical responsibility to practice, to the best of their ability, according to the standards of their profession. Nevertheless, the kinds of practices advocated in this position statement are more likely to be implemented within an infrastructure of supportive policies and resources. NAEYC strongly recommends that policy-making groups at the state and local levels consider the following when implementing early childhood programs:

1. A comprehensive professional preparation and development system is in place to ensure that early childhood programs are staffed with qualified personnel (NAEYC 1994).

   - A system exists for early childhood professionals to acquire the knowledge and practical skills needed to practice through college-level specialized preparation in early childhood education/child development.

   - Teachers in early childhood programs are encouraged and supported to obtain and maintain, through study and participation in inservice training, current knowledge of child development and learning and its application to early childhood practice.

   - Specialists in early childhood special education are available to provide assistance and consultation in meeting the individual needs of children in the program.

- In addition to management and supervision skills, administrators of early childhood programs have appropriate professional qualifications, including training specific to the education and development of young children, and they provide teachers time and opportunities to work collaboratively with colleagues and parents.

2. Funding is provided to ensure adequate staffing of early childhood programs and fair staff compensation that promotes continuity of relationships among adults and children (Willer 1990).

   - Funding is adequate to limit the size of the groups and provide sufficient numbers of adults to ensure individualized and appropriate care and education. Even the most well-qualified teacher cannot individualize instruction and adequately supervise too large a group of young children. An acceptable adult–child ratio for four- and five-year-olds is two adults with no more than 20 children (Ruopp et al. 1979; Francis & Self 1982; Howes 1983; Taylor & Taylor 1989; Howes, Phillips, & Whitebook 1992; Cost, Quality, & Child Outcomes Study Team 1995; Howes, Smith, & Galinsky 1995). Younger children require much smaller groups. Group size and ratio of children to adults should increase gradually through the primary grades, but one teacher with no more than 18 children or two adults with no more than 25 children is optimum (Nye et al. 1992; Nye, Boyd-Zaharias, & Fulton 1994). Inclusion of children with disabilities may necessitate additional adults or smaller group size to ensure that all children's needs are met.

   - Programs offer staff salaries and benefits commensurate with the skills and qualifications required for specific roles to ensure the provision of quality services and the effective recruitment and retention of qualified, competent staff. (See *Compensation Guidelines for Early Childhood Professionals* [NAEYC 1993].)

   - Decisions related to how programs are staffed and how children are grouped result in increased opportunities for children to experience continuity of relationships with teachers and other children. Such strategies include, but are not limited to, multiage grouping and multiyear teacher–child relationships (Katz, Evangelou, & Hartman 1990; Zero to Three 1995; Burke 1996).

3. Resources and expertise are available to provide safe, stimulating learning environments with a sufficient number and variety of appropriate materials and equipment for the age group served (Bronson 1995; Kendrick, Kaufmann, & Messenger 1995).

4. Adequate systems for regulating and monitoring the quality of early childhood programs are in place (see position on licensing [NAEYC 1987]; accreditation criteria and procedures [NAEYC 1991]).

5. Community resources are available and used to support the comprehensive needs of children and families (Kagan 1991; NASBE 1991; Kagan et al. 1995; NCSL 1995).

6. When individual children do not make expected learning progress, neither grade retention nor social promotion are used; instead, initiatives such as more focused time, individualized instruction, tutoring, or other individual strategies are used to accelerate children's learning (Shepard & Smith 1989; Ross et al. 1995).

7. Early childhood programs use multiple indicators of progress in all development domains to evaluate the effect of the program on children's development and learning and regularly report children's progress to parents. Group-administered, standardized, multiple-choice achievement tests are not used before third grade, preferably before fourth grade. When such tests are used to demonstrate public accountability, a sampling method is used (see Shepard 1994).

REFERENCES

Adams, G. & Sandfort, J. (1994). *First Steps, Promising Futures: State Prekindergarten Initiatives in the Early 1990s*. Washington, DC: Children's Defense Fund.

Alexander, K. L. & Entwisle, D. R. (1988). *Achievement in the First 2 Years of School: Patterns and Processes*. Monographs of the Society for Research in Child Development, vol. 53, no. 2, serial no. 218. Ann Arbor: University of Michigan.

Arnett, J. (1989). Caregivers in day-care centers: Does training matter? *Journal of Applied Developmental Psychology* 10(4): 541–52.

Asher, S., Hymel, S. & Renshaw, P. (1984). Loneliness in children. *Child Development* 55: 1456–64.

Barnett, W. S. (1995). Long-term effects of early childhood programs on cognitive and school outcomes. *The Future of Children* 5(3): 25–50.

Bergen, D. (1988). *Play as a Medium for Learning and Development.* Portsmouth, NH: Heinemann.

Berk, L. E. (1996). *Infants and Children: Prenatal through Middle Childhood.* (2nd ed.). Needham Heights, MA: Allyn & Bacon.

Berk, L. & Winsler, A. (1995). *Scaffolding Children's Learning: Vygotsky and Early Childhood Education.* Washington, DC: NAEYC.

Berrueta-Clement, J. R., Schweinhart, L. J., Barnett, W. S., Epstein, A. S. & Weikart, D. P. (1984). *Changed lives: The Effects of the Perry Preschool Program on Youths through Age 19.* Monographs of the High/Scope Educational Research Foundation, no. 8. Ypsilanti, MI: High/Scope Press.

Bodrova, E. & Leong, D. (1996). *Tools of the Mind: The Vygotskian Approach to Early Childhood Education.* Englewood Cliffs, NJ: Merrill/Prentice Hall.

Bowlby, J. (1969). *Attachment and Loss: Attachment.*, vol. 1. New York: Basic.

Bowman, B. (1994). The challenge of diversity. *Phi Delta Kappan* 76(3): 218–25.

Bowman, B. & Stott, F. (1994). Understanding development in a cultural context: The challenge for teachers. In *Diversity and Developmentally Appropriate Practices: Challenges for Early Childhood Education,* eds. B. Mallory & R. New, 119–34. New York: Teachers College Press.

Bredekamp, S., ed. (1987). *Developmentally Appropriate Practice in Early Childhood Programs Serving Children from Birth through Age 8.* (Exp. ed.). Washington, DC: NAEYC.

Bredekamp, S. (1993a). Reflections on Reggio Emilia. *Young Children* 49(1): 13–17.

Bredekamp, S. (1993b). The relationship between early childhood education and early childhood special education: Healthy marriage or family feud? *Topics in Early Childhood Special Education* 13(3): 258–73.

Bredekamp, S. & Rosegrant, T., eds. (1992). *Reaching Potentials: Appropriate Curriculum and Assessment for Young Children,* vol. 1. Washington, DC: NAEYC.

Bredekamp, S. & Rosegrant, T., eds. (1995). *Reaching Potentials: Transforming Early Childhood Curriculum and Assessment,* vol. 2. Washington, DC: NAEYC.

Bronfenbrenner, U. (1979). *The Ecology of Human Development: Experiments by Nature and Design.* Cambridge, MA: Harvard University Press.

Bronfenbrenner, U. (1989). Ecological systems theory. In *Annals of Child Development,* vol. 6, ed. R. Vasta, 187–251. Greenwich, CT: JAI Press.

Bronfenbrenner, U. (1993). The ecology of cognitive development: Research models and fugitive findings. In *Development in Context,* eds. R. H. Wozniak & K. W. Fischer, 3–44. Hillsdale, NJ: Erlbaum.

Bronson, M. B. (1995). *The Right Stuff for Children Birth to 8: Selecting Play Materials to Support Development.* Washington, DC: NAEYC.

Brophy, J. (1992). Probing the subtleties of subject matter teaching. *Educational Leadership* 49(7): 4–8.

Bruner, J. S. (1983). *Child's Talk: Learning to Use Language.* New York: Norton.

Bruner, J. S. (1996). *The Culture of Education*. Cambridge, MA: Harvard University Press.

Bryant, D. M., Clifford, R. & Peisner, E. S. (1991). Best practices for beginners: Developmental appropriateness in kindergarten. *American Educational Research Journal* 28(4): 783–803.

Burchinal, M., Robert, J. Nabo, L. & Bryant, D. (1996). Quality of center child care and infant cognitive and language development. *Child Development* 67(2): 606–20.

Burke, D. (1996). Multi-year teacher/student relationships are a long overdue arrangement. *Phi Delta Kappan* 77(5): 360–61.

Caine, R. & Caine, G. (1991). *Making Connections: Teaching and the Human Brain*. New York: Addison-Wesley.

Campbell, F. & Ramey, C. (1995). Cognitive and school outcomes for high-risk African-American students at middle adolescence: Positive effects of early intervention. *American Educational Research Journal* 32(4): 743–72.

Carnegie Task Force on Learning in the Primary Grades. (1996). *Years of Promise: A Comprehensive Learning Strategy for America's Children*. New York: Carnegie Corporation of New York.

Carta, J., Schwartz, L., Atwater, J. & McConnell, S. (1991). Developmentally appropriate practice: Appraising its usefulness for young children with disabilities. *Topics in Early Childhood Special Education* 11(1): 1–20.

Case, R. & Okamoto, Y. (1996). *The Role of Central Conceptual Structures in the Development of Children's Thought*. Monographs of the Society of Research in Child Development, vol. 61, no. 2, serial no. 246. Chicago: University of Chicago Press.

Charlesworth, R., Hart, C. H., Burts, D. C. & DeWolf, M. (1993). The LSU studies: Building a research base for developmentally appropriate practice. In *Perspectives on Developmentally Appropriate Practice: Advances in Early Education and Day Care*, vol. 5, ed. S. Reifel, 3–28. Greenwich, CT: JAI Press.

Chugani, H., Phelps, M. E. & Mazziotta, J. C. (1987). Positron emission tomography study of human brain functional development. *Annals of Neurology* 22(4): 495.

Cohen, N. & Modigliani, K. (1994). The family-to-family project: Developing family child care providers. In *The Early Childhood Career Lattice: Perspectives on Professional Development*, eds. J. Johnson & J. B. McCracken, 106–10. Washington, DC: NAEYC.

Copple, C., Sigel, I. E. & Saunders, R. (1984). *Educating the Young Thinker: Classroom Strategies for Cognitive Growth*. Hillsdale, NJ: Erlbaum.

Cost, Quality, & Child Outcomes Study Team. (1995). *Cost, Quality, and Child Outcomes in Child Care Centers, Public Report*. (2nd ed.). Denver: Economics Department, University of Colorado at Denver.

Dana Alliance for Brain Initiatives. (1996). *Delivering Results: A Progress Report on Brain Research*. Washington, DC: Author.

DEC/CEC (Division for Early Childhood of the Council for Exceptional Children). (1994). Position on inclusion. *Young Children* 49(5): 78.

DEC (Division for Early Childhood) Task Force on Recommended Practices. (1993). *DEC Recommended Practices: Indicators of Quality in Programs for Infants and Young Children with Special Needs and their Families*. Reston, VA: Council for Exceptional Children.

DEC/CEC & NAEYC (Division for Early Childhood of the Council for Exceptional Children & the National Association for the Education of Young Children). (1993). *Understanding the ADA—The Americans with Disabilities Act: Information for Early Childhood Programs*. Pittsburgh, PA & Washington, DC: Authors.

DeVries, R. & Kohlberg, W. (1990). *Constructivist Early Education: Overview and Comparison with Other Programs*. Washington, DC: NAEYC.

Dewey, J. (1916). *Democracy and Education: An Introduction to the Philosophy of Education*. New York: Macmillan.

Durkin, D. (1987). A classroom-observation study of reading instruction in kindergarten. *Early Childhood Research Quarterly* 2(3): 275–300.

Durkin, D. (1990). Reading instruction in kindergarten: A look at some issues through the lens of new basal reader materials. *Early Children Research Quarterly* 5(3): 299–316.

Dweck, C. (1986). Motivational processes affecting learning. *American Psychologist* 41: 1030–48.

Dyson, A. H. & Genishi, C. (1993). Visions of children as language users: Language and language education in early childhood. In *Handbook of Research on the Education of Young Children*, ed. B. Spodek, 122–36. New York: Macmillan.

Edwards, C. P. & Gandini, L. (1989). Teachers' expectations about the timing of developmental skills: A cross-cultural study. *Young Children* 44 (4): 15–19.

Edwards, C., Gandini, L. & Forman, G. eds. (1993). *The Hundred Languages of Children: The Reggio Emilia Approach to Early Childhood Education*. Norwood, NJ: Ablex.

Erikson, E. (1963). *Childhood and society*. New York: Norton.

Feeney, S. & Kipnis, K. (1992). *Code of Ethical Conduct & Statement of Commitment*. Washington, DC: NAEYC.

Fein, G. (1981). Pretend play: An integrative review. *Child Development* 52: 1095–118.

Fein, G. & Rivkin, M. eds. (1986). *The Young Child at Play: Reviews of Research*. Washington, DC: NAEYC.

Fenson, L., Dale, P., Reznick, J. S., Bates, E., Thal, D. & Pethick, S. (1994). *Variability in Early Communicative Development*. Monographs of the Society for Research in Child Development, vol. 59, no. 2, serial no. 242. Chicago: University of Chicago Press.

Fernald, A. (1992). Human maternal vocalizations to infants as biologically relevant signals: An evolutionary perspective. *In The Adapted Mind: Evolutionary Psychology and the Generation of Culture*, eds. J. H. Barkow, L. Cosmides, & J. Tooby, 391–428. New York: Oxford University Press.

Fields, T., Masi, W., Goldstein, S., Perry, S. & Parl, S. (1988). Infant day care facilities preschool social behavior. *Early Childhood Research Quarterly* 3(4): 341–59.

Forman, G. (1994). Different media, different languages. In *Reflections on the Reggio Emilia Approach*, eds. L. Katz & B. Cesarone, 37–46. Urbana, IL: ERIC Clearinghouse on EECE.

Forman, E. A., Minick, N. & Stone, C. A. (1993). *Contexts for Learning: Sociocultural Dynamics in Children's Development*. New York: Oxford University Press.

Francis, P. & Self, P. (1982). Imitative responsiveness of young children in day care and home settings: The importance of the child to caregiver ratio. *Child Study Journal* 12: 119–26.

Frede, E. (1995). The role of program quality in producing early childhood program benefits. *The Future of Children* 5(3): 115–132.

Frede, E. & Barnett, W. S. (1992). Developmentally appropriate public school preschool: A study of implementation of the High/Scope curriculum and its effects on disadvantaged children's skills at first grade. *Early Childhood Research Quarterly* 7(4): 483–99.

Fromberg, D. (1992). Play. In *The Early Childhood Curriculum: A Review of Current Research* (2nd ed.), ed. C. Seefeldt, 35–74. New York: Teachers College Press.

Galinsky, E., Howes, C., Kontos, S. & Shinn, M. (1994). *The Study of Children in Family Child Care and Relative Care: Highlights of Findings*. New York: Families and Work Institute.

Gallahue, D. (1993). Motor development and movement skill acquisition in early childhood education. In *Handbook of Research on the Education of Young Children*, ed. B. Spodek, 24–41. New York: Macmillan.

Gallahue, D. (1995). Transforming physical education curriculum. *In Reaching Potentials: Transforming Early Childhood Curriculum and Assessment*, vol. 2, eds. S. Bredekamp & T. Rosegrant, 125–44. Washington, DC: NAEYC.

Garbarino, J., Dubrow, N., Kostelny, K. & Pardo, C. (1992). *Children in Danger: Coping with the Consequences of Community Violence*. San Francisco: Jossey-Bass.

Gardner, H. (1983). Frames of Mind: *The Theory of Multiple Intelligences*. New York: Basic.

Gardner, H. (1991). *The Unschooled Mind: How Children Think and How Schools Should Teach*. New York: Basic.

Gelman, R. & Baillargeon, R. (1983). A review of some Piagetian concepts. In *Handbook of Child Psychology*, vol. 3, ed. P. H. Mussen, 167–230. New York: Wiley.

Gelman, R. & Meck, E. (1983). Preschoolers' counting: Principles before skill. *Cognition* 13: 343–59.

Hale-Benson, J. (1986). *Black Children: Their Roots, Cultures, and Learning Styles*. (Rev. ed.). Baltimore: Johns Hopkins University Press.

Herron, R. & Sutton-Smith, B. (1971). *Child's Play*. New York: Wiley.

Hiebert, E. H. & Papierz, J. M. (1990). The emergent literacy construct and kindergarten and readiness books of basal reading series. *Early childhood Research Quarterly* 5(3): 317–34.

Hohmann, M. & Weikart, D. (1995). *Educating Young Children: Active Learning Practices for Preschool and Child Care Programs*. Ypsilanti, MI: High/Scope Educational Research Foundation.

Hollestelle, K. (1993). At the core: Entrepreneurial skills for family child care providers. In *The Early Childhood Career Lattice: Perspectives on Professional Development*, eds. J. Johnson & J. B. McCracken, 63–65. Washington, DC: NAEYC.

Howes, C. (1983). Caregiver behavior in center and family day care. *Journal of Applied Developmental Psychology* 4: 96–107.

Howes, C. (1988). Relations between early child care and schooling. *Developmental Psychology* 24(1): 53–57.

Howes, C., Phillips, D. A., & Whitebook, M. (1992). Thresholds of quality: Implications for the social development of children in center-based child care. *Child Development* 63(2): 449–60.

Howes, C., Smith, E. & Galinsky, E. (1995). *The Florida Child Care Quality Improvement Study*. New York: Families and Work Institute.

Kagan, S. L. (1991). *United we Stand: Collaboration for Child Care and Early Education Services*. New York: Teachers College Press.

Kagan, S., Goffin, S., Golub, S. & Pritchard, E. (1995). *Toward Systematic Reform: Service Integration for Young Children and their Families*. Falls Church, VA: National Center for Service Integration.

Kamii, C. & Ewing, J. K. (1996). Basing teaching on Piaget's constructivism. *Childhood Education* 72(5): 260–64.

Katz, L. (1995). *Talks with Teachers of Young Children: A Collection*. Norwood, NJ: Ablex.

Katz, L. & Chard, S. (1989). *Engaging Children's Minds: The Project Approach*. Norwood, NJ: Ablex.

Katz, L., Evangelou, D. & Hartman, J. (1990). *The Case for Mixed-age Grouping in Early Education*. Washington, DC: NAEYC.

Kendrick, A., Kaufmann, R. & Messenger, K. eds. (1995). *Healthy Young Children: A Manual for Programs*. Washington, DC: NAEYC.

Kohn, A. (1993). *Punished by Rewards*. Boston: Houghton Mifflin.

Kostelnik, M., Soderman, A. & Whiren, A. (1993). *Developmentally Appropriate Programs in Early Childhood Education*. New York: Macmillan.

Kuhl, P. (1994). Learning and representation in speech and language. *Current Opinion in Neurobiology* 4: 812–22.

Lary, R.T. (1990). Successful students. *Education Issues* 3(2): 11–17.

Layzer, J. I., Goodson, B. D. & Moss, M. (1993). *Life in Preschool: Observational Study of Early Childhood Programs for Disadvantaged Four-year-olds*, vol. 1. Cambridge, MA: Abt Association.

Lazar, I. & Darlington, R. (1982). *Lasting Effects of Early Education: A Report from the Consortium for Longitudinal Studies*. Monographs of the Society for Research in Child Development, vol. 47, nos. 2–3, serial no. 195. Chicago: University of Chicago Press.

Lee, V. E., Brooks-Gunn, J. & Schuur, E. (1988). Does head start work? A 1-year follow-up comparison of disadvantaged children attending Head Start, no preschool, and other preschool programs. *Developmental Psychology* 24(2): 210–22.

Legters, N. & Slavin, R. E. (1992). Elementary students at risk: A status report. Paper commissioned by the Carnegie Corporation of New York for meeting on elementary-school reform. 1–2 June.

Levy, A. K., Schaefer, L. & Phelps, P. C. (1986). Increasing preschool effectiveness: Enhancing the language abilities of 3- and 4-year-old children through planned sociodramatic play. *Early Childhood Research Quarterly* 1(2): 133–40.

Levy, A. K., Wolfgang, C. H. & Koorland, M. A. (1992). Sociodramatic play as a method for enhancing the language performance of kindergarten age students. *Early Childhood Research Quarterly* 7(2): 245–62.

Malaguzzi, L. (1993). History, ideas, and basic philosophy. In *The Hundred Languages of Children: The Reggio Emilia Approach to Early Childhood Education*, eds. C. Edwards, L. Gandini, & G. Forman, 41–89. Norwood, NJ: Ablex.

Mallory, B. (1992). Is it always appropriate to be developmental? Convergent models for early intervention practice. *Topics in Early Childhood Special Education* 11(4): 1–12.

Mallory, B. (1994). Inclusive policy, practice, and theory for young children with developmental differences. In *Diversity and Developmentally Appropriate Practices: Challenges for Early Childhood Education*, eds. B. Mallory & R. New, 44–61. New York: Teachers College Press.

Mallory, B. L. & New, R. S. (1994a). *Diversity and Developmentally Appropriate Practices: Challenges for Early Childhood Education*. New York: Teachers College Press.

Mallory, B. L. & New, R. S. (1994b). Social constructivist theory and principles of inclusion: Challenges for early childhood special education. *Journal of Special Education* 28(3): 322–37.

Marcon, R. A. (1992). Differential effects of three preschool models on inner-city 4-year-olds. *Early Childhood Research Quarterly* 7(4): 517–30.

Maslow, A. (1954). *Motivation and Personality*. New York: Harper & Row.

Miller, L. B. & Bizzell, R. P. (1984). Long-term effects of four preschool programs: Ninth and tenth-grade results. *Child Development* 55(4): 1570–87.

Mitchell, A., Seligson, M. & Marx, F. (1989). *Early Childhood Programs and the Public Schools*. Dover, MA: Auburn House.

Morrow, L. M. (1990). Preparing the classroom environment to promote literacy during play. *Early Childhood Research Quarterly* 5(4): 537–54.

NAEYC. (1987). *NAEYC Position Statement on lLicensing and Other Forms of Regulation of Early Childhood Programs in Centers and Family Day Care*. Washington, DC: Author.

NAEYC. (1991). *Accreditation Criteria and Procedures of the National Academy of Early Childhood Programs*. (Rev. ed.). Washington, DC: Author.

NAEYC. (1993). *Compensation Guidelines for Early Childhood Professionals*. Washington, DC: Author.

NAEYC. (1994). NAEYC position statement: A conceptual framework for early childhood professional development, adopted November 1993. *Young Children* 49(3): 68–77.

NAEYC. (1996a). NAEYC position statement: Responding to linguistic and cultural diversity—Recommendations for effective early childhood education. *Young Children* 51(2): 4–12.

NAEYC. (1996b). NAEYC position statement: Technology and young children—Ages three through eight. *Young Children* 51(6): 11–16.

NAEYC & NAECS/SDE (National Association of Early Childhood Specialists in State Departments of Education). (1992). Guidelines for appropriate curriculum content and assessment in programs serving children ages 3 through 8. In *Reaching Potentials: Appropriate Curriculum and Assessment for Young Children*, vol. 1, eds. S. Bredekamp & T. Rosegrant, 9–27. Washington, DC: NAEYC.

NASBE (National Association of State Boards of Education). (1991). *Caring Communities: Supporting Young Children and Families*. Alexandria, VA: Author.

Natriello, G., McDill, E. & Pallas, A. (1990). *Schooling Disadvantaged Children: Racing Against Catastrophe*. New York: Teachers College Press.

NCES (National Center for Education Statistics) (1993). *The Condition of Education, 1993*. Washington, DC: US Department of Education.

NCSL (National Conference of State Legislatures) (1995). *Early Childhood Care and Education: An Investment that Works*. Denver: Author.

NEGP (National Education Goals Panel) (1991). *National Education Goals Report: Building a Nation of Learners*. Washington, DC: Author.

New, R. (1993). Cultural variations on developmentally appropriate practice: Challenges to theory and practice. In *The Hundred Languages of Children: The Reggio Emilia Approach to Early Childhood Education*, eds. C. Edwards, L. Gandini, & G. Forman, 215–32. Norwood, NJ: Ablex.

New, R. (1994). Culture, child development, and developmentally appropriate practices: Teachers as collaborative researchers. In *Diversity and Developmentally Appropriate Practices: Challenges for Early Childhood Education*, eds. B. Mallory & R. New, 65–83. New York: Teachers College Press.

Nye, B. A., Boyd-Zaharias, J. & Fulton, B. D. (1994). *The Lasting Benefits Study: A Continuing Analysis of the Effect of Small Class Size in Kindergarten through Third Grade on Student Achievement Test Scores in Subsequent Grade Levels—Seventh Grade (1992–93), Technical Report*. Nashville: Center of Excellence for Research in Basic Skills, Tennessee State University.

Nye, B. A., Boyd-Zaharias, J., Fulton, B. D. & Wallenhorst, M. P. (1992). Smaller classes really are better. *The American School Board Journal* 179(5): 31–33.

Parker, J. G. & Asher, S. R. (1987). Peer relations and later personal adjustment: Are low-accepted children at risk? *Psychology Bulletin* 102(3): 357–89.

Phillips, C. B. (1994). The movement of African-American children through sociocultural contexts: A case of conflict resolution. In *Diversity and Developmentally Appropriate practices: Challenges for Early Childhood Education*, eds. B. Mallory & R. New, 137–54. New York: Teachers College Press.

Phillips, D. A., McCartney, K. & Scarr, S. (1987). Child care quality and children's social development. *Developmental Psychology* 23(4): 537–43.

Piaget, J. (1952). *The Origins of Intelligence in Children*. New York: International Universities Press.

Plomin, R. (1994a). *Genetics and Experience: The Interplay Between Nature and Nurture*. Thousand Oaks, CA: Sage.

Plomin, R. (1994b). Nature, nurture, and social development. *Social Development* 3: 37–53.

Powell, D. (1994). Parents, pluralism, and the NAEYC statement on developmentally appropriate practice. In *Diversity and Developmentally Appropriate Practices: Challenges for Early Childhood Education*, eds. B. Mallory & R. New, 166–82. New York: Teachers College Press.

Pramling, I. (1991). Learning about "the shop": An approach to learning in preschool. *Early Children Research Quarterly* 6(2): 151–66.

Resnick, L. (1996). Schooling and the workplace: What relationship? In *Preparing Youth for the 21st Century*, 21–27. Washington, DC: Aspen Institute.

Rogoff, B. (1990). *Apprenticeship in Thinking: Cognitive Development in Social Context*. New York: Oxford University Press.

Rogoff, B., Mistry, J., Goncu, A. & Mosier, C. (1993). *Guided Participation in Cultural Activity by Toddlers and Caregivers*. Monographs of the Society for Research in Child Development, vol. 58, no. 8, serial no. 236. Chicago: University of Chicago Press.

Ross, S. M., Smith, L. J., Casey, J. & Slavin, R. E. (1995). Increasing the academic success of disadvantaged children: An examination of alternative early intervention programs. *American Educational Research Journal* 32(4): 773–800.

Ruopp, R., Travers, J., Glantz, J. & Coelen, C. (1979). *Children at the Center: Final Report of the National Day Care Study*. Cambridge, MA: ABT Associates.

Sameroff, A. & McDonough, S. (1994). Educational implications of developmental transitions: Revisiting the 5- to 7-year shift. *Phi Delta Kappan* 76(3): 188–93.

Scarr, S. & McCartney, K. (1983). How people make their own environments: A theory of genotype—environment effects. *Child Development* 54: 425–35.

Schrader, C. T. (1989). Written language use within the context of young children's symbolic play. *Early Childhood Research Quarterly* 4(2): 225–44.

Schrader, C. T. (1990). Symbolic play as a curricular tool for early literacy development. *Early Childhood Research Quarterly* 5(1): 79–103.

Schweinhart, L. J. & Weikart, D. P. (1996). *Lasting Differences: The High/Scope Preschool Curriculum Comparison Study through Age 23.* Monographs of the High/Scope Educational Research Foundation, no. 12. Ypsilanti, MI: High/Scope Press.

Schweinhart, L. J., Barnes, H. V. & Weikart, D. P. (1993). *Significant Benefits: The High/Scope Perry Preschool Study through Age 27.* Monographs of the High/Scope Educational Research Foundation, no. 10. Ypsilanti, MI: High/Scope Press.

Schweinhart, L. J., Weikart, D. P. & Larner, M. B. (1986). Child-initiated activities in early childhood programs may help prevent delinquency. *Early Childhood Research Quarterly* 1(3): 303–12.

Seefeldt, C., ed. (1992). *The Early Childhood Curriculum: A Review of Current Research* (2nd ed.). New York: Teachers College Press.

Seifert, K. (1993). Cognitive development and early childhood education. In *Handbook of Research on the Education of Young Children*, ed. B. Spodek, 9–23. New York: Macmillan.

Seppanen, P. S., Kaplan deVries, D. & Seligson, M. (1993). *National Study of Before and After School Programs.* Portsmouth, NH: RMC Research Corp.

Shepard, L. (1994). The challenges of assessing young children appropriately. *Phi Delta Kappan* 76(3): 206–13.

Shepard, L. A. & Smith, M. L. (1988). Escalating academic demand in kindergarten: Some nonsolutions. *Elementary School Journal* 89(2): 135–46.

Shepard, L. A., & Smith, M. L. (1989). *Flunking Grades: Research and Policies on Retention.* Bristol, PA: Taylor & Francis.

Slavin, R., Karweit, N. & Madden, N. eds. (1989). *Effective Programs for Students at-Risk.* Boston: Allyn & Bacon.

Smilansky, S. & Shefatya, L. (1990). *Facilitating Play: A Medium for Promoting Cognitive, Socioemotional, and Academic Development in Young Children.* Gaithersburg, MD: Psychosocial & Educational Publications.

Spodek, B., ed. (1993). *Handbook of Research on the Education of Young Children.* New York: Macmillan.

Sroufe, L. A., Cooper, R. G. & DeHart, G. B. (1992). *Child Development: Its Nature and Course.* (2nd ed.). New York: Knopf.

Stern, D. (1985). *The Psychological World of the Human Infant.* New York: Basic.

Stremmel, A. J. & Fu, V. R. (1993). Teaching in the zone of proximal development: Implications for responsive teaching practice. *Child and Youth Care Forum* 22(5): 337–50.

Taylor, J. M. & Taylor, W. S. (1989). *Communicable Diseases and Young Children in Group Settings.* Boston: Little, Brown.

Tobin, J., Wu, D. & Davidson, D. (1989). *Preschool in Three Cultures.* New Haven, CT: Yale University Press.

US Department of Health & Human Services (1996). *Head Start Performance Standards.* Washington, DC: Author.

Vandell, D. L. & Corasanti, M. A. (1990). Variations in early child care: Do they predict subsequent social, emotional, and cognitive differences? *Early Childhood Research Quarterly* 5(4): 555–72.

Vandell, D. L. & Powers, C. D. (1983). Day care quality and children's free play activities. *American Journal of Orthopsychiatry* 53(4): 493–500.

Vandell, D. L., Henderson, V. K. & Wilson, K. S. (1988). A longitudinal study of children with day-care experiences of varying quality. *Child Development* 59(5): 1286–92.

Vygotsky, L. (1978). *Mind in Society: The Development of Higher Psychological Processes.* Cambridge, MA: Harvard University Press.

Wardle, F. (1996). Proposal: An anti-bias and ecological model for multi-cultural education. *Childhood Education* 72(3): 152–56.

Wertsch, J. (1985). *Culture, Communication, and Cognition: Vygotskian Perspectives.* New York: Cambridge University Press.

White, S. H. (1965). Evidence for a hierarchical arrangement of learning processes. In *Advances in Child Development and Behavior,* eds. L. P. Lipsitt & C. C. Spiker, 187–220. New York: Academic Press.

Whitebook, M., Howes, C. & Phillips, D. (1989). *The National Child Care Staffing Study: Who Cares? Child Care Teachers and the Quality of Care in America.* Final report. Oakland, CA: Child Care Employee Project.

Wieder, S. & Greenspan, S. L. (1993). The emotional basis of learning. In *Handbook of Research on the Education of Young Children,* ed. B. Spodek, 77–104. New York: Macmillan.

Willer, B. (1990). *Reaching the Full Cost of Quality in Early Childhood Programs.* Washington, DC: NAEYC.

Willer, B., Hofferth, S. L., Kisker, E. E., Divine-Hawkins, P., Farquhar, E. & Glantz, F. B. (1991). *The Demand and Supply of Child Care in 1990.* Washington, DC: NAEYC.

Witkin, H. (1962). *Psychological Differentiation: Studies of Development.* New York: Wiley.

Wolery, M. & Wilbers, J. eds. (1994). *Including Children with Special Needs in Early Childhood Programs.* Washington, DC: NAEYC.

Wolery, M., Strain, P. & Bailey, D. (1992). Reaching potentials of children with special needs. In *Reaching Potentials: Appropriate Curriculum and Assessment for Young Children,* vol. 1, eds. S. Bredekamp & T. Rosegrant, 92–111. Washington, DC: NAEYC.

Zero to Three: The National Center (1995). *Caring for Infants and Toddlers in Groups: Developmentally Appropriate Practice.* Arlington, VA: Author.

PROFESSIONAL ORGANIZATIONS

When looking to further your development, a professional organization is a great place to start. There are several organizations, some of which even have state or local affiliates.

National Association for the Education of Young Children (NAEYC)
1509 16th Street, NW
Washington DC 20036
800-424-2460
www.naeyc.org
Email membership@naeyc.org

Specific membership benefits
Comprehensive Members receive all the benefits of Regular membership described below plus annually receive five or six books immediately after their release by NAEYC.

Regular and Student Members receive

- six issues of *Young Children*, which includes timely articles on pertinent issues, as well as suggestions and strategies for enhancing children's learning

- reduced registration fees at NAEYC-sponsored local and national conferences and seminars

- discounted prices on hundreds of books, videos, brochures and posters from NAEYC's extensive catalog of materials

- access to the *Members Only* Web site, including links to additional resources and chat sites for communication with other professionals.

National Association of Child Care Professionals (NACCP)
P.O. Box 90723
Austin, TX 78709
800-537-1118
www.naccp.org

Specific membership benefits

Management Tools of the Trade™

Your membership provides complete and FREE access (a $79 value) to these effective management tools that provide technical assistance in human resource management. In addition, members will receive NACCP's quarterly trade journals, **Professional Connections©**, **Teamwork©**, and **Caring for Your Children©**, to help you stay on top of hot issues in child care. Each edition also includes a Tool of the Trade™.

National Child Care Association (NCCA)
1016 Rosser St.
Conyers GA 30012
800-543-7161
www.nccanet.org

Specific membership benefits

- as the only recognized voice in Washington DC, NCCA has great influence on our legislators

- professional development opportunities are available

Association for Education International (ACEI)
The Olney Professional Building
17904 Georgia Avenue, Suite 215
Olney, MD 20832
Phone: 800-423-2563 or 301-570-2122
Fax: 301-570-2212
Web site: http://www.acei.org

ACEI is an international organization dedicated to promoting the best educational practices throughout the world.

Specific membership benefits

- workshops and travel/study tours abroad

- four issues per year of the journal *Childhood Education* and the *Journal of Research in Childhood Education*

- hundreds of resources for parents and teachers, including books, pamphlets, audiotapes, and video tapes.

National AfterSchool Association (NAA)
1137 Washington Street
Boston, MA 02124
Phone: 617-298-5012
Fax: 617-298-5022
Web site: http://www.naaweb.org

NAA is a national organization dedicated to providing information, technical assistance, and resources concerning children in out-of-school programs. Members include teachers, policy-makers, and administrators representing all public, private, and community-based sectors of after-school programs.

Specific member benefits

- a subscription to the NAA journal, *School-Age Review*

- a companion membership in state affiliates

- discounts on NAA publications and products

- discount on NAA annual conference registration

- opportunity to be an NAA accreditation endorser

- public policy representatives in Washington, DC

OTHER ORGANIZATIONS TO CONTACT

The Children's Defense Fund
25 E. St. NW
Washington DC 20001
202-628-8787
www.childrensdefense.org

National Association for Family Child Care
P.O. Box 10373
Des Moines, IA 50306
800-359-3817
www.nafcc.org
Journal: *The National Perspective*

National Black Child Development Institute
1023 15th Ave. NW
Washington DC 20002

202-833-2220
www.nbcdi.org

National Head Start Association
1651 Prince Street
Alexandria VA 22314
703-739-0875
www.nhsa.org
Journal: *Children and Families*

International Society for the Prevention of Child Abuse
and Neglect
25 W. 560 Geneva Road, Suite L2C
Carol Stream, IL 60188
630-221-1311
http://www.ispcan.org
Journal: *Child Abuse and Neglect: The International Journal*

Council for Exceptional Children
1110N. Glebe Road, Suite 300,
Arlington, VA 22201
888-CEC-SPED
www.cec.sped.org
Journal: *CEC Today*

National Association for Bilingual Education
Union Center Plaza
810 First Street, NE
Washington DC 20002
www.nabe.org
Journal: *NABE Journal of Research and Practice*

International Reading Association
800 Barksdale Road
P.O. Box 8139
Newark, DE 19714
800-336-READ
www.reading.org
Journal: *The Reading Teacher*

National Education Organization (NEA)
1201 16th St. NW
Washington, DC 20036
202-833-4000
www.nea.org
Journals: *Works4Me* and *NEA Focus*, by online subscription.

Zero to Three: National Center for Infants, Toddlers, and Families
2000M. Street NW, Suite 200
Washington DC 20036
202-638-1144
www.zerotothree.org
Journal: *Zero to Three*

RESOURCES

BOOKS

Aycox, F. (1997). *Games We should Play in School* (2nd ed.) Discovery Bay: Front Row Experience.

Bailey, B. (1997). *There's Gotta Be a Better Way: Discipline That Works!* Ovieda: Loving guidance, Inc.

Bergstrom, J. M. (1984). *School's Out.* Berkeley: Ten Speed Press.

Bittinger, G. (1994). *Teaching Snacks: Teaching Basic Concepts & Skills through Cooking.* Everest, WA: Warren Publishing House.

Cole, R. (1992). *Their Eyes Meeting the World: The Drawings and Paintings of Children.* Boston: Houghton Mifflin.

Dietz, W. H. & Stern, L. (eds.) (1999). *American Academy of Pediatrics Guide to Your Child's Nutrition: Making Peace at the Table and Building Healthy Eating Habits for Life.* New York: Villard.

Fink, D. B. (1995). *Discipline in School-Age Care: Control the Climate, Not the Children.* Nashville: School-Age NOTES.

Haas-Foletta, K. & Cogley, M. (1990). *School-Age Ideas and Activities for After-School Programs.* Nashville: School-Age NOTES.

Kasser, S. L. (1995). *Inclusive Games: Movement for Everyone!* Champaign: Human Kinetics.

Lewis, B. (1995). *The Kid's Guide to Service Projects.* Minneapolis: Free Spirit Publishing.

Miller, K. (1996). *The Crisis Manual: How to Handle the Really Difficult Problems.* Beltsville: Gryphon House.

Moore, A. C. (1992). *The Game Finder: A Leader's Guide to Great Activities*. State College: Venture Publishing.

Newman, R. L. (1998). *Building Relationships with Parents and Families in School-Age Programs*. Nashville: School-Age NOTES.

Patten, E. & Lyons, K. (2003). *Healthy Foods from Healthy Soils: A Hands-on Resource for Educators*. Gardiner, ME: Tilbury House.

Scofield, R. (ed.) (2001). *Summer Program Tips: Strategies and Activities*. Nashville: School-Age NOTES.

Tinsley, B. J. (2003). *How Children Learn to Be Healthy*. New York: Cambridge University Press.

Wallace, E. (1994). *Summer Sizzlers and Magic Mondays: School-Age Theme Activities*. Nashville: School-Age NOTES.

Warner, P. (1994). *Healthy Treats and Super Snacks for Kids*. Chicago: Contemporary Books.

Whitaker, D. L. (1996). *Games, Games, and Games: Creating Hundreds of Group Games and Sports*. Nashville: School-Age NOTES.

INTERNET RESOURCES

American Academy of Pediatrics
http://www.aap.org
Although much of the information on this site is for pediatricians or other health practitioners, you can access links to information about child care settings and the children in your care.

The American Library Association
http://www.ala.org
Search for Public Information Office > Choose Press Kits > Choose Library Card Sign Up Month 2002
Links to resources for children to find good Web sites to visit and view recommended reading and software. Parents will find information on adult reference and media materials as well as a link to Booklist magazine.

Child Care Aware
http://www.childcareaware.org
This resource can help parents find an appropriate setting for their children. The site lists Child Care Resource and Referral Services (CCR & Rs) throughout the US.

Public Playground Safety (formerly Handbook for Public Playground Safety)

http://www.cpsc.gov

Choose CPSC Publications > Playground Safety

Multiple publications are available online from the Consumer Product Safety Commission.

Healthy Child Care

http://www.healthychild.net

Healthy Childcare is a bimonthly publication devoted to health and safety issues. The Web site includes an online library of articles from past issues, suggestions for activities, and links to other sites.

National Child Care Information Center

http://www.nccic.org

NCCIC is a service of the Child Care Bureau, part of the US Department of Health and Human Services. The organization is a clearinghouse and technical assistance center that links parents, providers, policy-makers, researchers, and the public to child care and education information. Topics include nutrition, fatherhood, early literacy, and including children with disabilities.

US Department of Agriculture Food & Nutrition Information Center

http://www.nal.usda.gov

Choose Services and Programs > Food and Nutrition Information Center >.Child Care Nutrition Resource System

Information about nutrition and help in planning menus, cooking with children, and food safety measures. This site also has links to other Web sites that provide information about children's health and well-being. You can also find the Child Care Nutrition Resource System, which includes information on food safety, food preparation, and recipes. Links to other helpful resources for those working in USDA's Child Nutrition Programs.

National Resource Center for Health & Safety in Child Care

http://nrc.uchsc.edu

Clearinghouse for information on health and safety in child care. Topics include licensing requirements for each state plus suggestions for health strategies.

National Safe Kids Campaign

http://www.safekids.org

Community-based activities that promote child passenger safety and prevent childhood accidents. The organization also provides safety tips and information about product recalls. There is a link to activities for children to teach safety.

US General Services Administration (GSA)
Afterschool.gov
http://www.afterschool.gov
One-stop access to government resources for information about after-school issues and programs. Children will also find many safe and interesting government Web sites that help them navigate the many governmental sources of information. Children can find help with homework projects, jobs, volunteer opportunities, and much more.

COMPUTER PROGRAMS FOR CHILDREN

The choice of computer programs or other media for any group of children should be made on the basis of the make-up of the group, their needs, and their particular interests. The following Internet sources provide information about programs for you to review before choosing any for the children in your care. Some also offer information about movies and books.

http://www.superkids.com
Reviews new software and has games to increase vocabulary, logic, and reasoning. Also available are a Reading Corner that lists award-winning books for pre-readers, young readers, teens, and parents, as well as a Movie Corner with a vast selection of classics and family favorites.

http://www.muohio.edu
Search for dragonfly
Science information for upper-elementary children designed by the National Science Teachers Association and the National Science Foundation with students at Miami University Center for Human Development, Learning and Teaching at Miami. Provides opportunities for children to participate in inquiry-based learning. Some of the topics include: butterflies, baseball in space, time, water, earth sounds, and many more. There is information for research purposes and interactive games for children to hone their skills.

http://www.juniornet.com
This is an online service for children. Here children can play challenging games, work puzzles, and learn new arts and craft activities. The site also provides safe email access to children.

http://www.knowledgeadventure.com

Knowledge Adventure© has a wide range of software from different sources as well as a special page for educators. Includes product reviews and demonstration programs that can be downloaded.

http://softwareforkids.com

Software for children from preschool to middle school. Parents and teachers will find educational software to help children master essential concepts, and develop problem-solving and critical thinking skills.

VIDEOS FOR CAREGIVERS

Appropriate Curriculum for Young Children: The Role of the Teacher

(28 minutes)

Shows adults helping children learn through play and child-initiated activities.

New Games for Child Care Settings

(28 minutes)

Simple games that are non-competitive and build skills for preschool and school-age children.

Before- and After-School Creative Experiences

(28 minutes)

Shows how children can develop independence in a safe environment and with the support of adults.

National Association for the Education of Young Children (NAEYC)
Phone: (800) 424-2460
Fax: (202) 328-2649
http://www.naeyc.org

How to lead Games

(39 minutes)

Viewers are shown how to divide teams and are offered a formula for teaching new games. The material demonstrates a variety of games for all ages, using strategies that reinforce positive play and team building.

School-Age Notes
Phone: (800) 410-8780

Keys to Quality in School-Age Child Care

(25 minutes)

Four separate segments:
Key 1—Plan with School-Age Children in Mind
Key 2—Organize for Diversity and Choice (focusing on space and
        varied activities, scheduling, and staffing)
Key 3—View Parents as Partners with Programs
Key 4—Collaborate with others who can help

Roberta Newman, Newroads Consulting
Phone: (757) 331-3151
Email: Newroads_consulting@earthlink.net

Links to Learning: Supporting Literacy in Out-of-School Time

(12 minutes)

Highlights ways caregivers can promote literacy within the activities and curriculum.

A Place of Their Own: Designing Space for Out-of-School Time

(15 minutes)

Shows effective strategies for planning space for out-of-school programs; includes accompanying guide.

Making the Most of Out-of-School Time: The Human Side of Quality

(11 minutes)

Shows the importance of the relationships that develop in out-of-school programs.

Available from:
Ruth Kropf
Phone: (781) 283-2510
http://www.niost.org
Choose Publications > Videos

The plans that went awry: You have planned to have the children make music instruments as a craft activity. The children will take two paper cups and place small pebbles, rice, or beans in one, then tape the two cups together at the tops and then use the instruments as part of music time. It was just after Easter when you did the materials purchasing for this activity. You found some cute cups with bunnies and eggs on them at a clearance price. You have the activity set up on the art table ready for the children to begin work. Six-year-old Nicky sits at the table, picks up one of the cups and says, "I'm Jewish! I'm not making one!" What do you do? *This situation is one of many in which you will develop awareness and sensitivity to issues surrounding diversity. Whenever planning any curriculum activity, it is a good idea to ask yourself if the activity is sensitive to the cultural make-up of your class. In this particular situation, Nicky can probably be easily pacified by giving him two plain cups to use for making his shaker. Have other cups available for other children as well.*

Jeremy, a seven-year-old in your after-school program, has been playing handball for 40 minutes. There are six children waiting for a turn to play. What do you do? You could tell Jeremy that it is time to let other children have a turn, which might make him quick to anger and cause him to yell at you, calling you a very sexually derogatory name. Now what? *There are two issues to this scenario. The first issue is Jeremy's method of dealing with his feelings. The second is the verbal abuse directed to you, the caregiver. Your response can acknowledge Jeremy's feelings, tell him that it is inappropriate language, and give him alternative language that would be more appropriate. Jeremy's feelings were not taken into consideration and he got angry. "Jeremy, I can see that you are angry. You wanted to play handball longer. Do you remember that we talked about how each person needs to limit his playing time so more children can play?" Then, quietly go to Jeremy, pull him aside and walk with him until he calms down. Once he is calmer, tell him that the words he used when he was angry are words that hurt feelings and are not appropriate for young boys to use. Ask him what might be other words he can use when he is angry. Finally, tell Jeremy that in the future, you will give him a warning so he knows his turn is just about over. He should also be told that if he continues to use inappropriate language the consequence will be that he spend time isolated from his friends and that his parents will be called for a conference. That said, however, the original problem is a child-owned problem. The other children want a turn to play. When you attempt to solve the problem, you have robbed the children of the opportunity to solve the problem themselves and you become the judge. Someone is going to lose. It is best if there can be a win–win situation. This is accomplished through negotiations. "Jeremy, stop playing handball for a few minutes. There is a problem. There are six children waiting for a turn to play. How are all of you going to solve this problem?" Encourage children to brainstorm solutions. The children will come up with an idea that works for them. Jeremy can save face by being part of the solution, not just part of the problem. Try not to fall into the trap of trying to solve the problem.*

Mrs. Hernandez comes to pick up her daughter, Juanita, from the after-school program. She seems visibly distraught and seeks you out. She tells you that she has just had a conference with Juanita's elementary teacher and Juanita is not doing well in school. She is behind in both reading and math. Mrs. Hernandez tells you that she wants Juanita to study the entire time she is at the after-school program. This is not consistent with the program philosophy of providing care for children that meets their needs physically and socially as well as academically. What will you do? *It is extremely important that Mrs. Hernandez feels heard. "I hear that you are very concerned about Juanita's grades in school." Ask her if the teacher had any specific ideas about how the after-school program could help Juanita. Try to establish a three-way partnership with the teacher and the parent. Be especially careful about respecting the teacher–parent relationship. Ask the parent for permission to speak to the teacher about specific strategies to help Juanita with homework time. Avoid the easy trap of siding with the parent against the teacher or siding with the teacher against the parent. Once the parent is at ease, it will be easier to remind her of Juanita's needs for social interaction and physical activities and that you strive to provide developmental oppor-tunities for the whole child. Continue to discuss with Mrs. Hernandez that Juanita's academic work is equally important and you will do everything you can to help her.*

Brian, a kindergartener, has just started in your after-school child care program. He arrives, puts his backpack down, and fairly quickly begins playing with two other boys in the block area. Within a few minutes there is a conflict in the block area. Apparently one of the other boys doesn't want to give him Brian the car he wants. Brian stands up and quickly walks to his backpack, pulls out his cell phone and calls his mother announcing, "He won't give me the car!" Brian appears to be listening to his mother and then he hands you the telephone saying, "My mom wants to talk to you." What will you do? *There are two levels of responses to this scenario, one is the response to the parent and the other is the response to the child. The immediate issue is to deal with the parent. It will be important to listen to the parent's concern and acknowledge her feelings. It may sound something like, "I can under-stand your concern. I can assure you that I will help Brian resolve this conflict." The parent may want to know what you are going to do about the problem Brian is having. She will want to hear that you will acknowledge Brian's feelings and help him brainstorm a solution with the other child. It is important to acknowledge the parent but it is equally important to get back to your job of caring for children. Disengage as quickly as possible from the parent and attend to the children. This is a child-owned problem and the children will need your skills in helping them resolve the conflict. Use active listening and encourage problem-solving by the children. Help them use appropriate words to express their feelings.*

ISSUES AND TRENDS

ISSUES IN EARLY CHILDHOOD EDUCATION

Literacy

The ability to read and write is crucial to children's success in school and throughout their adult life. In child care, you will not be expected to teach children to read and write, but you can do a great deal toward supplementing and enhancing what they have learned in school.

What you can do to foster literacy

- read to the children frequently

- encourage children to talk about what is read

- provide a wide variety of books—picture books, poetry, humor, and reference

- periodically add new books for children to read

- tell stories and ask children to relate their own stories

- provide daily opportunities for children to write their names, letters, and simple words

- emphasize the beginning and ending letters of words

- talk about letters and their sounds

- encourage children to identify the sounds of letters or words

- involve children in activities that require reading, such as cooking or playing games

- provide daily opportunities for children to write for different purposes—stories, lists, messages, captions to artwork, poems, and reports

- provide a print-rich environment with signs, labels, name tags, and pictures with captions

- read poetry and encourage children to be familiar with rhyming sounds

- encourage children to write their own stories or poems

- model enjoyment of reading.

For further information about helping children to become literate, search these Web sites:

National Association for the Education of Young Children
http://www.naeyc.org

International Reading Association—
http://www.reading.org

Bullying

Children test their power and their place in a group by bullying others. Both children who bully and their victims are hurt by their behavior so it is important to find ways to stop the behavior and mitigate the damage.

What you can do

- Stop the bullying immediately. If necessary stand between the children who are the perpetrators and the ones who are the victims.

- Recite the rules or policies against bullying. "Calling someone names is against our rules." "I won't allow you to make fun of the way he talks."

- Include other children in the discussion of the incident. Let them talk about what they saw happening or what they might have done to stop the behavior. "Maybe you didn't know what to do? How do you think you might react next time this happens?"

- Support the child who has been bullied. Let him discuss how it felt, what he might do next time, and how you will support his efforts.

- If necessary, impose immediate consequences to those who continue to bully others. Make the consequences logical and related to the offense. For example, you might take away opportunities for the bully to participate in a group activity.

- Let bullies know that you will be aware of their behavior.

- Lead discussions at group time about bullying and what everyone can do about it.

- Encourage the group to write their own set of rules about bullying.

- Plan activities that help children build self-confidence.

- Be a role model for respecting both children and adults.

For further information about bullying, check out the Web site of the US Department of Health and Human Services anti-bullying program: http://stopbullyingnow.hrsa.gov

Environmental Violence

Children are exposed to violence in their everyday lives, either indirectly through the media or directly in their neighborhoods and in their families. They hear news broadcasts of killings in other countries or a shooting in a business, school, or supermarket. They may even have witnessed a shooting on their own street. Movies and TV portray killings and violence. Adults cannot be expected to completely shield children from these experiences, but they can help them cope with the feelings that result.

What you can do

- Be willing to listen to children when they want to talk about what they have seen or experienced.

- Reassure children. Sometimes when they hear about scary things, they worry about their own safety. Even though you cannot change the situation, you can reassure them that you and their parents will keep them safe. "Your mom and dad won't let that happen to you." "While you are here in child care, I will keep you safe."

- Clear up misconceptions about what they have seen on TV news broadcasts. Do not try to give all the information available, but find out what they saw or what they heard. Follow with small pieces of information.

- Help children learn alternatives to the use of violence they hear on the news. When they have heard about someone who was angry and shot people in a supermarket, say "I get really upset when people solve their problems by hurting innocent people." You can then remind them of times they were able to find ways to deal with their own anger by means other than fighting. "When you got mad at Jeffrey the other day, remember how you shouted at him, but didn't hit him?"

- Provide opportunities for children to work out their feelings about violence through play, art, writing stories, and other activities.

For more information about violence search these Web sites:

National Institute of Mental Health—
http://www.nimh.nih.gov/

American Psychological Association—
http://www.apa.org

Child Abuse

All states and the federal government have laws relating to child abuse that are designed to protect children from physical or emotional abuse, neglect or deprivation, and sexual abuse and exploitation. You need to know what those laws include and what your responsibility is. Know what to look for and what to do if abuse is suspected. Sometimes children say or do things that should warn adults, but the idea that a child could have been abused is so repugnant that the tendency is to ignore the signs. Therefore it is important to know the law and to be able to consider the signs of abuse.

You can watch for

- unusual marks such as burns, bruises, cuts, or fractures

- inadequate clothing for the weather or clothes that are unclean

- withdrawal or unresponsiveness to others

- disruptive behavior or "acting out"

- refusal to eat

- exaggerated fears

- unusual interest and awareness of sexual activities

- seductive behavior with adults

- fear of adults and reluctance to talk to adults.

When abuse is suspected, what should you do?

- keep a record of observations, including dates and time

- take photographs of injuries (caution: these photos cannot be used for any other purpose without the parents' permission)

- talk to other teachers, directors or professionals

- report the abuse to the local child protective services, the sheriff's or police department.

For more information, search these Web sites:

US Department of Health and Human Services— http://www.hhs.gov

National Clearinghouse on Child Abuse Information— http://nccanch.acf.hhs.gov

Ethics
"The NAEYC Code of Ethical Conduct offers guidelines for responsible behavior and sets forth a common basis for resolving the principle dilemmas encountered in early childhood care and education." This is a quote from Feeney, S. & Freeman, N.K. (1999). *Ethics and the Early Childhood Educator Using the NAEYC Code*. Washington, DC: NAEYC. Some of the following main points from that document follow; they should guide you in reacting to and managing the common situations you will encounter in your work with children, parents, and your colleagues.

Ethical Responsibilities to Children
Your primary responsibility as a caregiver is to provide a safe, nurturing, and responsive environment for children. In doing so, each child's uniqueness must be respected.

Caregivers and teachers

- remain current in their knowledge of requirements for children's care and education

- recognize each child's unique characteristics and needs

- include children with disabilities and provide access to support services as needed

- above all else, adults shall not harm any child

- seek input from families and other professionals in order to maximize the potential of every child to benefit from the program.

Ethical Responsibilities to Families

Caregivers share mutual responsibility for children's development with parents or any others who are involved with the children. There must be a collaborative relationship between home and school.

Caregivers

- foster a relationship of mutual trust with parents

- respect families' culture, language, and child-rearing decisions

- help families improve child-rearing skills and their understanding of their children's development

- allow parents to have access to their children's program setting

- inform parents and involve them in policy decisions when it is appropriate

- involve families in important decisions concerning their children

- maintain confidentiality and respect parents' rights to privacy

- use community resources and services that can support families.

Ethical Responsibilities to Colleagues

The main focus of this section is on establishing a caring and cooperative workplace in which each person is respected. Your main responsibility is to establish professional relationships that support productive work and meet professional needs.

Staff members

- develop relationships of respect, trust, and cooperation

- make full use of the expertise and training of all staff members

- have working conditions that are safe and supportive and based on written personnel policies

- are supported in efforts to meet professional needs and in professional development

- will be informed of areas where they do not meet program standards and are assisted in improving

Responsibility to Community and Society

Every child care facility operates within a community made up of families and other institutions whose main concern is the welfare of children. It is important that the program meets the needs of the community and cooperates with other agencies.

The child care program will

- provide the community with high quality, developmentally appropriate care for children

- be sensitive to cultural differences among the children's families

- support policies and laws that benefit children and families

- communicate openly about the kinds of services offered

- hire only persons who are competent

- report unethical behavior of a coworker or supervisor.